CONTENTS
. . . .

INTRODUCTION

· · · · · · · · · · · · · · · · ·

This 15-month guide has been designed and written to give a concise and accessible insight into both the nature of your star sign and the year ahead. Divided into two main sections, the first section of this guide will give you an overview of your character in order to help you understand how you think, perceive the world and interact with others and – perhaps just as importantly – why. You'll soon see that your zodiac sign is not just affected by a few stars in the sky, but by planets, elements and a whole host of other factors, too.

The second section of this guide is made up of daily forecasts. Use these to increase your awareness of what might appear on your horizon so that you're better equipped to deal with the days ahead. While this should never be used to dictate your life, it can be useful to see how your energies might be affected or influenced, which in turn can help you prepare for what life might throw your way.

By the end of these 15 months, these two sections should have given you a deeper understanding and awareness of yourself and, in turn, the world around you. There are never any definite certainties, but with an open mind you will find guidance for what might be, and learn to take more control of your own destiny.

THE CHARACTER OF THE TWINS

· · · · · · · · · · · · · · · · ·

Expect a triple dose of conversation, charisma and intellect from Geminians. Not usually satisfied with focusing on one thing at a time, these artful communicators will likely be Tweeting celebrities, texting colleagues and Snapchatting friends simultaneously without even breaking a sweat. Fortunately, they often have twice as much energy as everyone else, so won't usually have an issue keeping up with their active social lives. Lively and affable, Geminians are friends, or at least good acquaintances, with everyone around them. Frequently found fluttering from friend to friend, these social butterflies touch the lives of many.

Geminians crave constant mental stimulation, which is perhaps why they are well known for being intelligent. They are expert conversationalists and are formidable opponents in a debate. Yet, as much as Geminians are happy to lead or even dominate a conversation, they are also just as eager to listen. To satisfy their eternal curiosity, they can be keen on learning all the facts about a story that has captured their interest, be it serious news or the latest celebrity break-up. This love for knowledge can lead to Geminians learning many secrets, but their athletic approach to conversing could result in them running around and sharing what they've learned with everyone else. They would be wise to keep gossip to a minimum and perhaps apply their knack for narrative to writing, like fellow Geminians Arthur Conan Doyle and Salman Rushdie.

THE TWINS

Double the trouble or twice the fun? The Twins that represent Gemini can be an indication of many, and sometimes opposing, traits. Castor and Pollux were twin half-brothers from Greek mythology who have commonly been portrayed as the Gemini symbol. In some stories, Castor is thought to be mortal, while Pollux is immortal. When Castor dies, he is sent to the Underworld ruled by Hades, leaving Pollux in Olympus with the Gods. The light and dark of this tale is a perfect example of the two sides that many Geminians are commonly thought to display. Their moods are changeable, which may sometimes make them appear deceitful or two-faced, while their mutable quality makes them strong advocates of change. Whether it's changing their hair colour or even their postcode, these fluid beings are often unrecognisable from one day to the next. However, Geminians are fascinating characters to try and get to know.

MERCURY

Orbiting the Sun faster than any other planet in the Solar System, travel and speed are two associations that Geminians surely inherit from their ruling planet of Mercury. Named after the Roman god of communication, trickery and travel, winged Mercury is a perfect embodiment of air sign Gemini. The speed in which we travel and communicate is ever increasing, much to the joy of quick-thinking Geminians. Feeling the influence of Mercury, they favour instantly gratifying forms of interaction. However, texting, Tweeting and talking rapidly can mean that Geminians may not always think before they speak or press send. 'Mercury in retrograde' is a phrase that is often met with fearful faces, but what does it mean? Three times a year, Mercury seemingly begins to move backwards in Earth's sky and in relation to the other planets, and this is blamed for many communication, media, technology and travel failures or mix-ups. It's a good idea to focus on clarity during these times; precision can help to avoid misunderstandings.

ELEMENTS, MODES AND POLARITIES

Each sign is made up of a unique combination of three defining groups: elements, modes and polarities. Each of these defining parts can manifest themselves in good and bad ways, and none should be seen as a positive or a negative – including the polarities! Just like a jigsaw puzzle, piecing these groups together can help illuminate why each sign has certain characteristics and help us find a balance.

ELEMENTS

Fire: Dynamic and adventurous, signs with fire in them can be extroverted. Others are naturally drawn to them because of the positive light they give off, as well as their high levels of energy and confidence.

Earth: Signs with the earth element are steady and driven with their ambitions. They make for solid friends, parents or partners due to their grounded influence and nurturing nature.

Air: The invisible element that influences each of the other elements significantly, air signs will provide much-needed perspective to others with their fair thinking, verbal skills and key ideas.

Water: Warm in the shallows, but sometimes as freezing as ice. This mysterious element is essential to the growth of everything around it, through its emotional depth and empathy.

MODES

Cardinal: Pioneers of the calendar, cardinal signs jump-start each season and are the energetic go-getters.

Fixed: Marking the middle of the calendar, fixed signs firmly denote and value steadiness and reliability.

Mutable: As the seasons end, the mutable signs adapt and give themselves over gladly to the promise of change.

POLARITIES

Positive: Typically extroverted, positive signs take physical action and embrace outside stimulus in their life.

Negative: Usually introverted, negative signs value emotional development and experiencing life from the inside out.

GEMINI IN BRIEF

The table below shows the key attributes of Geminians. Use it for quick reference and to understand more about this fascinating sign.

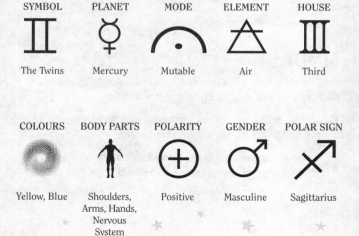

SYMBOL	RULING PLANET	MODE	ELEMENT	HOUSE
The Twins	Mercury	Mutable	Air	Third

COLOURS	BODY PARTS	POLARITY	GENDER	POLAR SIGN
Yellow, Blue	Shoulders, Arms, Hands, Nervous System	Positive	Masculine	Sagittarius

ROMANTIC RELATIONSHIPS

· · · · · · · · · · · · · · · · ·

Like their element of air, Geminians have a lightness to them that lifts others up. However, anyone who falls for these flyaway characters will need to work hard to keep their interests piqued. Geminians can reach dizzying heights of ecstasy in love but soon lose their curiosity, leaving partners plummeting back to Earth painfully. They are likely to have several possible love interests simultaneously, on multiple different dating apps, but may be quick to swipe left or abandon conversations if they get bored. Speed dating could be an interesting night out for this fast-paced chatterbox!

With a love of change and speed, Geminians may walk away from relationships too quickly. To hold onto a relationship, they will need to slow down and take a moment to honestly discuss whatever issues need to be mended. Nothing is perfect, and the most worthwhile endeavours are usually those that take time and effort – something that Geminians would do well to consider in their love lives. Whilst they are expert communicators, taking the time to pause and reflect on problems in a relationship will probably not come easily, and will be something they need to work hard at.

Not ones to take themselves too seriously, Geminians will appreciate energetic lovers that they can have fun with. Thanks to their mutable quality, they can be very easy-going in relationships and are unlikely to fight for the reins of control. They usually value partners who are similarly relaxed, but also could be attracted to more-forthright types who take the lead and encourage them to explore new heights. Keep curious Geminians intrigued and their love will be invigorating.

ARIES: COMPATIBILITY 4/5

Though very different in their approaches to relationships, these two positive signs can bring out the very best in one another. Communication is key for any relationship, and the Geminian's talkative nature can help the Arian to vocalise dreams and ideas. These two can form an intellectual bond that lays a strong foundation for love. The Twins and Ram are both guilty of starting projects and not finishing them, which can extend to their relationship with each other. However, their similarities and positive natures are likely to still see them part as friends if the romance extinguishes.

TAURUS: COMPATIBILITY 2/5

Three may prove to be a crowd. The duality of a Geminian, characterised in the Twin symbol, can make a Taurean feel uneasy about starting a romantic relationship. The earth sign of Taurus mixed with airy Gemini may not be an easy joining, but if the Taurean can budge on set ideas then love could grow happily here. The Geminian's good communication skills help when understanding the Taurean's needs, providing the love and security that is craved, while Taurus can help Gemini learn to take a calmer pace. Communication, trust and flexibility should be this couple's mantra if they are to go the distance.

GEMINI: COMPATIBILITY 4/5

A Geminian couple is likely to be a roaring hit at social gatherings. This pair can share late-night stimulating conversations until the early hours of the morning, and probably still be energised enough to make that brunch date. Life might feel like a constant party when two Geminians unite, but they may struggle to connect deeply on an emotional level. These smart thinkers match each other in many compatible ways, so this relationship will surely be full of shared thoughts and exciting adventures.

CANCER: COMPATIBILITY 2/5

This air and water pairing can feel too far apart personality-wise to make a good match, but in some cases the differences could actually prove to be strengthening. The Geminian is led by the mind and the Cancerian by emotion. These contrasting perspectives can lead to misunderstandings and arguments if the line of communication isn't clear. The Geminian can help the Cancerian communicate thoughts and feelings aloud rather than keeping them bottled up, while the Cancerian can provide lessons on the value of sensitivity. With so much to learn from one another, understanding and acceptance is vital to their success.

LEO: COMPATIBILITY 4/5

The inner Leonian child can be just what the youthful sign of Gemini asked for. This love can be like a children's story full of love and adventure; think Peter Pan and Wendy. The high-energy Leonian was born to lead, whilst the mutable Geminian is happy to take this Lion's hand and fly speedily off to Neverland! The Leonian will encourage the Geminian to take an active part in the important choices in their lives. Both positive signs, their extrovert energies and curious natures will see this air and fire match embarking on endless adventures.

VIRGO: COMPATIBILITY 1/5

A Virgoan may be attracted to a Geminian's charm and wit, but could soon feel irritated by the flights of fancy. The steady Virgoan can feel too reserved for the Geminian, and the fast-paced Geminian can be too much for the Virgoan. Both ruled by Mercury and strong believers in communication, these otherwise contrasting characters may end up feeling as if they are speaking two completely different languages. However, these signs combined are nothing if not unpredictable, and their mutual love of change and talent for adaptability may well be what makes this relationship go the distance.

AQUARIUS: COMPATIBILITY 4/5

An individualist Aquarian and dual-personality Geminian can make for a compatible trio. Born in the eleventh house, signifying community and friendship, the Aquarian thrives in groups and will be a fantastic partner to the social butterfly Geminian. Mutable in nature, the Geminian is happy to follow the Aquarian's fixed lead, which will likely bring a steadiness to the relationship. Both share the element of air and are positive, so are likely to have lots in common. With the Geminian's love of change and the Aquarian's need for progress, these two could create a bright and revolutionary future together.

PISCES: COMPATIBILITY 3/5

As fluid as water and as free flowing as air, a Piscean and Geminian can experience an extremely flexible and forgiving relationship if they fall for one another. Both mutable, this couple is highly compatible and will not fight for leadership, but rather rule side by side. Whilst these two may not always perfectly understand each other, their open-minded attitudes will help resolve any disagreements. Whilst the Geminian is led by the mind-influence of Mercury, contrastingly, the Piscean's influence of water means that they can both be ruled by their emotions. A meeting of heads and hearts will be key.

FAMILY AND FRIENDS

. . . .

'You think you know someone, and then you find out they're a Gemini'. That's the sentiment friends and family of Geminians may express. To truly know Geminians is to be able to identify their light and dark sides, their love of gossip and their passion for politics. Geminians should try to get to know both sides of themselves, just as much as their friends and family should. Their duality means they can be extremely good at acting as go-betweens to friends and families. Able to see two sides to every story, Geminians can act as a bridge of communication between two contrasting sides, making them potential peacemakers. Although they may instigate debates that turn into arguments, their knack for seeing multiple perspectives makes them a voice of reason that shouldn't be ignored.

Whether it's about global politics, last night's game or the food on their plate, Geminians will have an opinion about everything and love to debate it to the death. Not in it to win it, they have endless curiosity and enjoy being tested and presented with new ways of thinking, as this satisfies their love of learning. Rather than shy away from friends or family who challenge their intellect, stimulating relationships are ones that Geminians will usually try harder to hold on to. Be sure to bring the sparkliest conversation to one of their infamous dinner parties. However, if they fail to be entertained then they will move swiftly on, abandoning a dull conversation and searching quickly for something of more interest elsewhere. Geminians do not attempt to conceal their dwindling interest, so anyone wishing to hold their attention should watch closely – and be ready to change the subject!

FAMILY AND FRIENDS

Being related to Geminians, who carry the element of air, can sometimes feel like being caught up in a gale-force wind. Those closest will see them at their stormiest and strongest. Perhaps the quote often attributed to Geminian Marilyn Monroe best summed it up: "If you can't handle me at my worst, then you sure as hell don't deserve me at my best". Geminians talk non-stop and with endless energy, but if friends and family aren't left exhausted they will no doubt feel enlivened. Their need for constant change, even in relationships, may mean that the dynamics between family and friends constantly evolve and change too. Having the energy to keep up with Geminians mentally will be a task and a half, but can have exciting rewards. The young energy of Leonians makes them perfect playmates, whilst fellow Geminians are sure to make for more fun.

MONEY AND CAREERS

· · · · · · · · · · · · · · · · ·

Being a particular star sign will not dictate certain types of career, but it can help identify potential areas for thriving in. To succeed in the workplace, it is important to understand strengths and weaknesses, which will help in choosing and achieving career and financial goals.

The planet Mercury is thought to be able to change the way that people think, just like the influential Geminians who are ruled by it. These charismatic characters have a silver tongue and are more than capable of imprinting their intellect and ideas on those they encounter. They will likely have an aptitude for sales, but sometimes what they sell best is themselves. Kings, queens, prime ministers and presidents, Geminians have been ruling the world for decades. Strategy, intellect, communication and the desire and ability to create change are all defining features of Geminians and successful leaders. They have a great ability to multitask, so are usually best suited to a career that challenges them intellectually. Therefore, a career in politics is a strong potential avenue.

The youth associated with Mercury gives Geminians an eternal vitality, but could also mean that they are prone to making blunders. Fortunately, they love learning, so will usually grow from their mistakes. A teaching environment could be well suited to Geminians. Their ability to communicate and their influential way of thinking could make them favoured teachers amongst pupils. The annual changeover of students would also be a bonus for mutable Geminians, as long as the lessons themselves aren't too repetitive. They can become bored easily, so will not happily remain in a job that stays the same or prevents them from evolving in some way. Their love of words and narrative could mean that writing is where their talents best bloom, as with Geminian Salman Rushdie.

As with family, colleagues cannot be chosen. Therefore, it can be advantageous to use star signs to learn about their key characteristics and discover the best ways of working together. With the same element of Air, Librans and Aquarians will connect with Geminians on a thoughtful level, and can make inspiring and influential colleagues. Geminian Paul McCartney and Libran John Lennon are a great example of the dizzying heights of success that these two deep-thinkers can help each other reach. Steady Taureans are likely to lock horns with flighty Geminians over their advocacy for change in a work environment, and sometimes Geminians may be reluctant to engage with Taureans' more methodical approach. Both methods have their time to shine. An extra dollop of patience and understanding should be served up if they find themselves on the same team.

HEALTH AND WELLBEING

· · · · · · · · · · · · · · · · ·

Moved by their element air, Geminians are full of ideas and insights that will usually be heard loud and clear thanks to their influence of Mercury, the planet signifying communication. Conversely, if they feel like their voices are not being listened to, or are actively being silenced, their health and wellbeing will soon deteriorate. Whilst mutable Geminians are usually happy to go along with the plans of others, it's vital that they make their imprint in some way if they are to be true to themselves and feel content.

As much as Geminians advocate diversity in their lives and surroundings, they should similarly celebrate the complicated diversity within themselves. They can be accused of being dishonest, but their duality is an important part of their uniqueness that they should learn to embrace. Capable of being the life and soul of a party, Geminians can also be prone to feeling overwhelmed, and may sometimes need to take some space for themselves. Their social sides should be exercised as much as their quieter, more thoughtful aspects to help maintain emotional balance. Geminians should try to surround themselves with friends and family that allow them to show off their charming face and challenge their intellect, but don't require them to be always 'switched on'. Ultimately, they should strive to find a balance by making room to enjoy all sides of their changeable personalities.

Geminians can be eager to move on quickly from things, including their feelings. They like to remain light-hearted and can be guilty of skimming the surface only. Delving deeply into their emotions might initially feel suffocating to Geminians.

However, the practice of looking at their underlying emotions and desires can lead them away from living a purely shallow existence and bring a deeper resonance to their lives. By pausing and focusing more time and energy into themselves and their relationships, Geminians can often twice reap the rewards that they are used to receiving from their more impatient behaviour.

The part of the human body associated with Gemini is the nervous system. It ensures the body acts in the way that the brain tells it to, which is perhaps why communication is so closely connected to this sign. Geminians can push themselves mentally and physically to the point of exhaustion if they choose to ignore signals from their bodies telling them to slow down. However, they may find it difficult to listen to the warnings of pain and discomfort before damage is done. Whilst it is not in their nature to slow down, even energetic Geminians will tire eventually. They may be able to pre-empt a burnout by taking the time to switch off from the constant chatter of their outside life and focus on their internal health. Regular screen breaks and going offline from technology could give their overactive minds a much-needed rest. A peaceful retreat somewhere with terrible phone reception and no internet signal may be just what the doctor ordered.

Tuesday 5th

Pleasure is to be gained from a tidy home and a healthy body. Decluttering mess is the best thing you can do today. As the Moon shifts into your creative sector, you find that you have love in your heart for a tidy work space. Be proud of yourself.

Wednesday 6th

Yesterday's clutter was cleared just in time for the new moon in your creative sector. This is a busy day in the heavens, and you are asked to set an intention to put energy into transforming old things into something new and useful. Pluto, the transformer, goes direct today.

Thursday 7th

Venus moves into your relationship sector today. Here, she will bring beauty and harmony to strained relationships and initiate new, exciting ones. This blessing will enhance love connections that are built on a mutual need to explore the wider world. You can be optimistic about love for good reason now.

Friday 8th

The Sun meets Mars in your creative sector. The next three days will be highly passionate and driven. Your sex life will benefit from this energy too. There will be a great balance between your ego and divine self. The drive to express and receive back will be harmonised.

Saturday 9th

There's lots going on today. Sensual and emotional times with a partner are likely. The urge to say what's in your heart surfaces, but Mercury is in the heart of the Sun and demands that you listen to voices other than your own. Past loves may be remembered.

Sunday 10th

Saturn, your greatest teacher planet, now turns direct. A nod
from the Moon in your relationship sector thanks him for
the lessons about personal and collective boundaries. You are
feeling much more grounded and steadier than usual. Breathe
deeply and keep moving forwards.

Monday 11th

Today is a day of optimism and good humour. Relationships
go well and you may even be in favour with those above you.
This is a productive start to the week; prepare to step up your
game. This evening you are genuinely interested in building
something new for yourself. This could be a new career.

Tuesday 12th

You have come to realise that not all of your dreams need to be
hidden. Do you fear failure or exposure? There is no need. You
are admired for the way you think and process information and
today, this needs to come out into the open. Surprise yourself.

Wednesday 13th

You're probably wondering where this responsible side of you
has come from. You should know that you are not the airhead
you sometimes think you are. Major planetary shifts have
transformed your thinking and you now take yourself more
seriously. Go ahead and show the world what you're made of.

Thursday 14th

Travel and group adventures are likely coming back into your awareness. The Moon meets up with Saturn and your thirst for the wider world now has more substance. You may decide to involve a partner in this; think about how this could bond you deeper to each other.

Friday 15th

How can one person make a difference? This is what you are wondering now. Think big: something along the idea of a long-haul trip as a working volunteer may be calling to you. Jupiter is making sure that you know what you are doing. Do all the research again.

Saturday 16th

The Moon will be in your work sector all weekend and offers you the chance to take time to pause and reflect on your responsibilities. You are aware of how this area of life brings dissatisfaction and that change is needed. Use your skills to push forward and progress.

Sunday 17th

Jupiter now turns direct in your travel sector. You will experience this as a return of optimism and the need to reach out further into the world. You are willing to make huge changes now. Emotional pulls towards a dream career will keep your eye on the goal, however intangible it seems.

Monday 18th

Mercury turns direct now; this is always good news for a Gemini. Communications are lively, if a little self-serving. Put yourself out there; it's time to network and make your dream a reality. There's a green light giving you the go-ahead. Why wait?

Tuesday 19th

Your heart and mind have a talk and merge their ideals for your highest purpose. Understand that if your heart is yearning for something, then your eager mind will work out how to make it happen. You could feel a boost in enthusiasm and mental energy. Keep it simmering and do not burn out.

Wednesday 20th

A full moon in your fiery social sector acts as a huge light bulb or spotlight. You may even have a 'Eureka!' moment and find the best solution to your plans. Be aware that you may be emotionally charged and a little bit resistant, but this will pass.

Thursday 21st

From your hidden sector, the Moon connects to Saturn and this energy acts as a spot check. Make sure there is nothing you have overlooked. The monthly lunar visit to Uranus means that you can be unstable today. You may be like a dog trying to catch its own tail. Take a deep breath.

Friday 22nd

The Moon's connection to Neptune today may mean that you drift back into a fantasy world for a while. It is the weekend and there is a chance that you can over-do it when it comes to unhealthy or indulgent habits. Choose indulgences that bring calm; watch your favourite TV show or light a scented candle.

Saturday 23rd

The Sun moves into your health and duties sector as the Moon moves into your own sign and your sector of self. Use this energy to get in touch with your body and your overall health. Looking after yourself is of utmost importance now. Starting an exercise regime has a good chance of success.

Sunday 24th

The Moon opposes Venus who is sitting in your relationship sector. You will be torn between spending time by yourself and with another. This may cause some friction in your love life, so invite the 'other' to make suggestions on how to best take care of your own needs today.

Monday 25th

You have the necessary energy and motivation to get the working week off to a good start. Putting fragile and delicate dreams to one side may not be easy, but do so and you will become more productive. Be proud of yourself; your wandering mind can be tamed and focused for today.

Tuesday 26th

Get into the routine of rewarding yourself after a good day's work. Enjoy coming home to your own space and a favourite meal. However, there may be some uncomfortable feelings being pushed up from the depths of your psyche today. Take note of the triggers and listen to what these feelings say.

Wednesday 27th

It is possible that issues surrounding mothers and fathers, or your possessions and those you share with another, will arise. It is worth double-checking on your finances as there may be money owing that you have overlooked. Career dreams and your love life are likely to be at odds today.

Thursday 28th

You will be tempted to show off today. Your knowledge base is highly commended, but it is not always required. This can make you come across as a know-it-all and may cause tension with people in authority or in your wider social groups. Venus and Jupiter can help to smooth things over with a lover.

Friday 29th

Your gift of communication and thought-processing works well now. Say what you want with less vigour than yesterday and you will achieve more. You may surprise yourself, as this will hit a spot in your hidden sector that makes you sit up and take note. Learn from this.

Saturday 30th

Family may ask you to be flexible and need your attention today. This might be problematic as you have plans for yourself that you do not wish to amend. You must use your head and decide which would be the best course of action to take. Which will cause fewer problems?

Sunday 31st

Spending time with close family will make for a pleasant Sunday. Everyone around pulls together to make sure that chores get done, and no-one is overloaded. This could be a family get-together with surprises or unexpected good news. Be dutiful, join in and have fun with your nearest and dearest.

NOVEMBER

....

Monday 1st

As the week begins, you have another boost of motivation. The Moon sits opposite Neptune and you can see from afar how your daydreams and unrealistic goals have dragged you away from your responsibilities. Get creative with your travel plans and speak to others who have more experience.

Tuesday 2nd

Your ruler is getting you to question the nature of the changes you need to make. Mercury is helping you see a balanced way forward. Self-expression is easier now than is usually is, and you are likely to come up with some bold ideas. People will applaud you for this new approach.

Wednesday 3rd

You are in a space of time where you can merge both head and heart and come up with the ideal way for you to make progress. There will be an emotional wrench, which could involve needing to end something big before laying the fresh ground for new things to develop.

Thursday 4th

There is a new moon in your health and duties sector today. This Moon also connects to Mars, Uranus and Saturn. Whatever intentions you decide to make now will be fuelled by fairness, responsibility and the need to think outside the box. Someone important in your relationship sector needs your attention now.

Friday 5th

The Sun sits facing Uranus, and this can result in you feeling awkward and uneasy. Something you prefer to keep secret is under the spotlight now and you cannot escape confronting it. You may find the light shows that you've successfully dealt with something from your deepest parts and healed an old wound.

Saturday 6th

Mercury is now diving deep into your health and duties sector. Prepare for some investigation or detective work into recent health worries. Venus will also be probing deep into your intimacy sector. Together they will help you learn to put yourself first and work on making your boundaries healthier.

Sunday 7th

Spending time with a lover will help to put more things into perspective for you today. This may not be easy, but you must remember to put yourself first. If the 'other' cannot respect your personal boundaries, then they are not on the same page as you. If this is the case, consider what you want and need from this relationship.

Monday 8th

The Moon and Venus have a meet-up in your intimacy sector. They discuss how you must take the small steps to climb the highest mountain. If there is someone you wish to know better, then you must take it slowly and avoid burn-out. You will enjoy the slower pace now.

Tuesday 9th

The Moon meets Pluto and it is likely that you see a transformation today. The connection to Neptune suggests that you will see things from a different perspective. Neptune's fog lifts and you get more clarity. You may say goodbye to something which no longer serves you.

Wednesday 10th

There's a lot of difficult energy today. You may feel restricted or blocked at every turn. Perhaps leaders or teachers are not listening to what you have to say. This could get fraught, as Mars is part of this turbulent energy. Listen to your elders; don't react without thinking.

Thursday 11th

Today you can feel more outgoing and wish to connect to the wider world. It is possible that you join up with a group fighting for a good cause, such as a conservation project. This can fire you up to do something personally to help. You may be outraged at an injustice right now.

Friday 12th

Your wish to help others brings you back to thinking about your career progression. This is another time to pause and reflect. Look at the experience you already have. How can this be used now? What new skills would be useful for you to learn?

Saturday 13th

Today you really want to make a difference. You have a sense of an adventure akin to the search for the Holy Grail. You know it may never materialise, but you are thinking about dedicating yourself to the cause. Mercury is teasing this out of you and making you aware of it.

Sunday 14th

This new mission of yours could even be religious or spiritual in nature. This afternoon, the Moon enters your social sector and you may feel it would be a good idea to connect with groups to network and share ideas. You are driven and active now, your energy is high.

Monday 15th

You may have pushed a certain avenue too far. You are getting the nod from Venus that, although your enthusiasm is a good thing, it may have taken you down a route which is ultimately not good for you. Stop, breathe and evaluate the road so far.

Tuesday 16th

The Moon and Sun both connect to Pluto today and this can mean that control or power struggles have surfaced. Emotionally, you feel that this comes from your social sector, but it is more likely that something deep within you is struggling to be made conscious and you are denying it space.

Wednesday 17th

Your hidden sector is now visited by the Moon and you may feel that there is someone watching your every move. This is enhanced by Mars opposing Uranus, who both like to cause trouble. Be careful that you do not get aggressive today; there is still subconscious material surfacing.

Friday 26th

Again, you experience tension with an elder, leader or figure of authority. When the Moon is in your communication sector, your natural inclination to share information can be tainted with narcissism. Showing off will not get you anywhere. Time to exercise the other side of communication and use your ears.

Saturday 27th

Family time comes around for the weekend. Here is where you feel safe to say what is on your mind. However, you prefer to see order rather than chaos in your family connections, so you are able to tone it down. Make sure that you do not let others walk over you now.

Sunday 28th

Neptune and Uranus both connect to the Moon today. Your family time may be spent sharing dreams and visions. When you have a get together like this, you can talk around problems with confidence and compassion. You may be the one who finds a unique solution.

Monday 29th

You're probably feeling that it is time to get creative or passionate about a project or a love affair. However, your ruler, Mercury, is in the heat of the Sun and is blocked. You may feel this as brain fog and wonder why you are unable to think straight. Get physical instead.

Tuesday 30th

Today you are juggling with a lot of areas. You have scholarly opportunities to take and discussions to enjoy. At the same time, you are trying to deal with fantastical thinking about life's mysteries. Try looking for a spiritual group who can help you answer these questions for yourself.

DECEMBER

· · · · · · · · · · · · · · · ·

Wednesday 1st

Great news; Neptune turns direct today. All that ruminating you have been doing over a career change will now have more clarity. You must continue to listen to your inner voice as your guide. Use more instinct and intuition now rather than logic. This is your future calling.

Thursday 2nd

You do not have to be a martyr. Being of service to others is a virtue, but not when it becomes more important than looking after your own needs. Conflicted feelings will cause underlying tension, which may erupt if you are not practising self-care.

Friday 3rd

Today can be pretty tense for you. Do something physical to let off some steam, perhaps with a good workout at the gym. Alternatively, brainstorm some ideas and theories with someone close. This can get deep and heavy, but you will enjoy it. Love is favoured for the weekend as the Moon shifts into your relationship sector.

Saturday 4th

This is an excellent day for romance and renewing commitment to someone special. A new moon in your relationship sector introduces new beginnings in this area. Your ruler, Mercury, also gets in on the act and grants you the gift of meaningful conversation. No small talk, today.

Sunday 5th

Jupiter lends your relationships his optimism and wish for adventure today. Discussing travel opportunities with a loved one, looking at maps or watching documentaries will fill up your Sunday. You will begin taking the necessary steps to make a dream getaway into a reality. Enjoy this time with a kindred soul who thinks like you.

Monday 6th

Changing the way you have previously looked at something will reap rewards today. Intimacy will have a different meaning for you now. The energy is ripe for mutual bonds to deepen and transform a relationship. The Moon's first contact with newly direct Neptune brings attainable dreams at work.

Tuesday 7th

The Moon meets Pluto in your intimacy sector. This influence can sometimes bring control issues, but not today. You have taken the steps to make substantial changes in a difficult area of life. This is highly productive and brings you satisfaction. This afternoon, you are ready to share time with friends.

Wednesday 8th

You may feel strained or overwhelmed today. Don't worry, this will soon pass. You are reacting emotionally to the recent developments you have made. It is uncomfortable for you to be ruled by passion and not your mind. In this case, your mind does not matter.

Thursday 9th

If you are feeling stuck or hindered by people above you, lie low and just listen to what they have to say. Good advice can come from unlikely sources. You may feel victimised but, in fact, you are being guided towards the best possible path for you. Employ your passive listening skills.

Friday 10th

At work, you can be dreamy again and not fix on the task in hand. This changeable way of dealing with things is natural to you, which is why you often fall into it as a default action. Go with the flow, but do not overlook the important things.

Saturday 11th

Venus and Pluto meet up today. This influence can produce a seductive, intimate time in your love life, but beware of power games that could lead to one or both of you getting hurt. Be open and honest, and set some time to discuss boundaries, so neither of you drift too far away into a fantasy land.

Sunday 12th

There may be issues beyond your control within friendship groups today. You are outgoing and high spirited, but this may clash with others. Venus and Pluto are still together; they have the power to make great changes or endings together. A love connection can be transformed now.

Monday 13th

Mercury enters your intimacy sector now. Your ruler will help you have conversations that can sometimes be difficult or even taboo. Don't jump in too deep, and take baby steps. Mars enters your relationship sector; this could mean a super sexy time or an exhausting one. Use his energy wisely.

Tuesday 14th

The Moon slips into your hidden sector today. Get confident about sharing your deepest self with another. You can have a low image of yourself and feel you are unworthy. Do not hide away; you are allowed to enjoy the little luxuries of life out in the open, too.

Wednesday 15th

Why do you feel guilty? You are too hard on yourself right now. The Moon meets Uranus and you feel this like an intrusion into your private life. Saturn is making it even more difficult for you as he is reminding you of how far is too far. Pull back if you need to.

Thursday 16th

The Moon's connection to Venus and Pluto can make you uneasy if you let it. It is best that you recognise this energy of deep change in your hidden and intimate sectors as a need to be more open in relationships. Try to feel more and analyse less.

Friday 17th

You feel more like yourself, as the Moon hits familiar ground in your sector of self. In your own sign, you are more confident and outgoing. Reach out to the future and envisage a new you. Your inner compass is guiding you. There is high activity in your love life today.

Saturday 18th

Venus turns retrograde now in your intimacy sector. You may become reserved and turn your back on a loved one. You may also find it difficult to focus on the steps you need to climb on that mountain to success. Expect endings or the return of a lost love during this time.

Sunday 19th

As the festive season looms closer, a full moon in your own sign highlights all that you have been through this year. This is the perfect time to evaluate your journey so far. Celebrate your successes, mourn your losses and do not look back with regret.

Monday 20th

You may feel the need to stay in your own home today. The coming weeks can be exhausting, so use this time to get comfortable in your own space. Treat yourself to favourite foods and get your tribe around. You may have a heart versus head battle today, but this should be brief.

Tuesday 21st

The winter solstice arrives, and the longest night asks that you pause, reflect and still your mind. You may see some conflict between men and women in the family. Review your role as a responsible nurturer and think about those who nourish you. Give thanks for family love today.

Wednesday 22nd

Today you will probably be actively catching up with people. Perhaps the parties have already started. Phone calls, messages and short trips are likely. Be careful that you do not get drawn into an argument with a person from your social sector. Make sure all jobs are done today.

Thursday 23rd

Jupiter has returned to the final degree of your travel sector. He wants you to get out and explore the wider world but is asking you to make sure that there is nothing you have overlooked. Your inquisitive mind will be able to spot if there is something you need to attend to now.

Friday 24th

The Moon moves into your family sector just as the celebrations begin. There is touchy energy from the planets, suggesting that there will be a lot of people vying to take control of the festive activities. Stay away from the chaos, or use your gifts of communication to bring peace.

Saturday 25th

Venus has retrograded to meet Pluto once more. This can be awkward on a day where people have joined together to celebrate. Power and control can be an issue today. Mercury and Uranus bring lively chatter and surprises, but there is a chance that it will be less than ideal.

Sunday 26th

Today is less frenzied and you are able to find peace and balance. You may be called upon to mediate or host the entertainment. The Moon makes a nice connection to Venus and Pluto, suggesting that loving transformations can be achieved if they are worked at.

Monday 27th

Consider spending today alone or with a special person. Your creative sector is highlighted with good, assertive energy and responsibility. Maybe a clean-up is needed. Set the pace for the day and restore harmony to your home or your love relationships. Quality time alone will also help you quieten your mind today.

Tuesday 28th

Just as you thought it was all over, the planetary energy throws more tension at you. Venus retrograde may see you bringing a permanent end to something you have been working on stealthily. Make sure that this is not a knee-jerk reaction; there is no coming back from this.

Wednesday 29th

Massive Jupiter enters your work sector now. This will be beneficial to you over the next year. He will bring luck and optimism and enlarge everything he touches, including your workload. As you are prone to dreaming in this area, he can expand that too, so be careful what you wish for now.

Thursday 30th

Mercury and Pluto meet in your intimacy sector. You will find that your conversations become deeper and take on a darker edge. You are in a place where the mysteries of life are interesting you more than ever. Choose your teachers in this area wisely.

Friday 31st

The year ends with the Moon meeting the point of past actions. This is a great time to reflect on what karma you decide to leave behind you as the year ends. Emotions and actions will be high today in your relationships. Think back to what 2021 has taught you.

Gemini

. . . .

DAILY FORECASTS
for 2022

JANUARY

· · · · · · · · · · · · · · · · ·

Saturday 1st

Happy New Year and welcome to 2022. Start the year with some cosy partner time. You may feel at odds today and need comfort and optimism from outside sources. Worry about what the year holds another time. For now, rest, recharge or switch off with like-minded people.

Sunday 2nd

A new moon gives you the best opportunity to review your career goals. Set your intentions now. Include areas where you would love to delve deeper and those that could give your career a boost. Networking with wider groups may give you food for thought or an incentive to explore the wider world.

Monday 3rd

You may experience some challenges, possibly from an old relationship or your current one. Issues may surface and emotions could get intense. Watch out for a tendency to become too stubborn. Alternatively, it could be you coming under the influence of a stubborn person.

Tuesday 4th

If you are still emotionally attached to something that isn't good for you, consider letting it go. This may take some time to get used to but is the right thing to do. You may be unpredictable today as triggers deep in your psyche cause disturbances you'd rather not deal with. Get them up, acknowledge them and work on healing them.

Wednesday 5th

Use your energy and drive to connect to people you admire and love spending time with. Partner time can benefit from this as you may be feeling more outgoing and generous than usual. Midweek romance may be exactly what you need to distract from your private worries. Keep an open mind and heart.

Thursday 6th

Be adaptable today. As a Gemini, you are already rather good at this. You may be presented with a challenge and feel stuck. Check all the information and get advice from an elder or boss if you need to. Inspiration and optimism can be powerful driving forces for you.

Friday 7th

Recognise what needs your attention and what drains you. If a relationship is demanding, you may wish to escape and have alone time. Your inner compass is in sight and will let you know if your activities are in alignment with your core purpose or not. Lighten your load this year.

Saturday 8th

There still could be festive activities for you to enjoy. Friendship groups call you out and fill a need to let off steam with those you trust. You could be getting up to mischief, but you may also be devising plans for a worthy cause. Interest groups can be stimulating.

Sunday 9th

A ghost from the past may attempt to pull you back to them today. This can bring up angry feelings that are difficult to ignore. Money issues can be a problem now too, especially joint investments. A conflict between your ego and emotions may be uncomfortable this evening.

Monday 10th

Check that a goal you've been chasing is still worth your energy. You may find that something is too far out of reach for you. It could be that a veil has been lifted and you have more clarity. What may have looked like a good idea once, no longer does.

Tuesday 11th

This is an unsettling day. You may have rumblings within you but you're not sure why. Restless energy can make communication unclear and you may be unusually stubborn. Relationships, both personal and business, may suffer from scattered focus. Use the energy to do something physical or practical, such as exercise.

Wednesday 12th

Staying grounded should lead to a more peaceful day. There may be some relief around money or past relationship stress. Take a look at your inner compass and imagine yourself at true north. Your emotions may be intense but in a positive way, which helps you stay in control.

Thursday 13th

The Moon in your sign settles your mind and allows you to see where your next steps on your personal journey are. It's possible that you have a moment of genius and can begin researching or learning something new. Don't commit to anything just yet, though, as Mercury retrogrades tomorrow.

Friday 14th

Make all the usual Mercury retrograde preparations today.
Back up all devices, double check travel plans and refrain
from signing anything binding. This will affect your
deepest emotions and money you may share with another.
Communications need to be crystal clear now. Get a clear head
for any mental activities.

Saturday 15th

Your love life may need more of your attention today, but you
have things to do. Try this afternoon when the mood changes
and you may feel more like being pampered or nurtured by
another. Nourish your body, mind and soul with things that
have quality and meaning to you.

Sunday 16th

Be incredibly careful today. The planetary energy is highly
unstable. You may witness a permanent ending in the
workplace. A new cycle is certainly beginning. However,
there is also something that is refusing to shift. An opinion
or standpoint may need to be reviewed as it isn't helping you
make progress.

Monday 17th

You may see a change that can be upsetting for you as it may
rock your sense of security. Power struggles may occur. A full
moon highlights what you need around you to be comfortable.
You could be gathering your resources or hoarding
unnecessary items as a way to cope.

Tuesday 18th

Uranus turns direct today, and this may mean that excavations in your psyche are now easier to deal with. A healing process can begin. Conversations or networking may not work well, and you may get frustrated at not being able to make yourself understood. Hold tight as this energy will pass soon.

Wednesday 19th

Try not to clash with an elder or person in authority. You must remember that they have boundaries as well as you. It could be that you are voicing unwanted opinions or delving into something that doesn't concern you. Life may feel limiting but use this as planning time.

Thursday 20th

You may be more outgoing and selfless now. The solar shift may open your heart a little more. Good causes or humanistic issues may attract you. You could be yearning for family life or be picking up your natural role again after the holidays. Decluttering would be good.

Friday 21st

Practical activity keeps your momentum going. You may be more methodical now and doing paperwork or coming to terms with your inner worries. Solutions may come and you can put these to good use. You are also more compassionate and tolerant towards people who may be clinging to your light.

Saturday 22nd

Your dreams may seem far away today, but this is probably a sign that mundane duties and family life need your attention more. You could find simple changes beneficial. A simple clear out can freshen up your home and make space for something new. Use your creative side this weekend.

Sunday 23rd

Listen out for any messages, hints or lessons that may be of use. You may have a sudden urge to be romantic or create something beautiful. Is there something regarding your personal relationships that needs one last push to accomplish? Aim for balance and harmony and stay away from chaos.

Monday 24th

You may now have more motivation and reason to deepen a love relationship by getting to know them better. This may be a slow process but if you can stay grounded it will be highly beneficial to both of you. It may be that the balance needs to be tipped first.

Tuesday 25th

This is an intense day where you may be run ragged with all your mundane duties. There may be feelings of jealousy or resentment. Watch out for triggers today as you may come across something that reopens old wounds. Go easy on yourself and take time to heal before you act.

Wednesday 26th

With two planets in retrograde in your intimacy zone, you'd be wise to be more of an observer now. Listen without speaking, hear without judging and above all don't react. You may feel deeply about this, but must pause and reflect before you make any kind of response.

Thursday 27th

You could be thinking about the past and making yourself believe that they were better times. If a person you were connected with is making a reappearance, remember that they may have no place in your present. You may be outgoing and motivated, but always remain true to yourself and core values.

Friday 28th

The world seems a little larger now. There may still be limits or restrictions imposed on you, but you can see around them and understand why they are there. Respectful and responsible actions can connect you to the wider world without breaching personal boundaries on either side. Reach out with kindness.

Saturday 29th

It's possible that you have resolved an issue from the past or are beginning to. Venus turns direct today and lightens your load. You may hear something to your advantage that can also help you to transform or heal a wound. You have the right energy to do this today.

Sunday 30th

Your compassion is boundless now as you may be able to negotiate a harmonic outcome to a problem. This may surprise you and those involved. Nevertheless, you could be pleased by your adult responses and feel that you have done what aligns with your truth and vision for the future.

Monday 31st

Today may have an emotional edge that is deep and intense. It could be that you receive news of something that could be life-changing in your career. It may be something that needs a total overhaul or review. Either way, this can be felt at your very core and you are moved.

FEBRUARY

....

Tuesday 1st

Today's new moon lets you set goals and intentions regarding exploring your world. You may wish to travel or learn about other cultures. It could be that you desire to be of more use and wish to lend your voice to activist causes. Release your inner rebel.

Wednesday 2nd

You may be feeling your way around new territory at work. If you have a new role or project, it's ok to research around it before hitting the road running. You have enough interest and energy for this, and you may find that it breathes new life into your career.

Thursday 3rd

With Jupiter in your career sector, you may expect your prospects to broaden. Joy, optimism and motivation in your work will be a theme while he is here. You may get an emotional attachment to the tasks you do. A boost of this helps you to enjoy a day of surprises.

Friday 4th

Mercury turns direct today. Review any issues that surfaced recently before committing yourself fully. You may find that you are in total alignment with your deepest wishes and feel like celebrating. Get your friends together and have a supercharged fun time. You could blaze a trail today.

Saturday 5th

After a busy, productive week, you may feel a little drained today and unable to do anything much. Maybe this is a good time to catch up with online courses or binge-watch favourite TV shows. Catching up with friends you don't talk to often will also be satisfying. Reach out to those who inspire you.

Sunday 6th

Today you may need to do something that feels tiresome or boring. This may be a necessary amendment to a project that has been lately revised. You could also feel that after delving deeply into a relationship recently, you need to pause for breath.

Monday 7th

It may take all day for your energy to pick up to a reasonable pace. However, when it does, you may work into the night on something that has piqued your interest. Personal work may be done now with good effect. Set your mind to finding practical solutions.

Tuesday 8th

Take it slowly today. Make deliberate steps towards progress and you will be unlikely to mess up. This evening you have a chance to put a dream to the test and see whether it's attainable or unrealistic. You may look at it with new eyes and discard anything you think is unlikely to work.

Wednesday 9th

You are a typical Gemini today. Your mood and mind may wander and not fix on any one thing. Use your mental powers to research, network and make decisions. If you need advice, don't hesitate to ask; it will be seen as you being keen to learn.

Thursday 10th

If things don't go your way at work, think of it as a challenge. You may be upset by injustice but look at all the factors. You may be missing vital bits of information so double-check all your resources. Communicating any concerns are a good way to show professionalism.

Friday 11th

You may get a breakthrough now and have more clarity about work or relationships. This could be the start of a thorough clean-up of things that no longer serve your best interests. You may need to have a difficult conversation with someone special. Remember to be kind.

Saturday 12th

Mars and Venus are getting closer in your intimacy sector. You may notice that one-to-one relationships are deepening. You may also see that you are merging your masculine and feminine sides and discovering the compassionate warrior within. Now is the time to go after what you desire with all your heart.

Sunday 13th

You could feel extra protective or defensive of your possessions and immediate environment today. If you feel under attack, retreat. Quality is important to you and makes you feel safe and secure. Do what feeds your soul, and protect those closest to you, too.

Monday 14th

The challenges you are experiencing make you more sensitive now. Try not to let this affect your work; if you do, you could well end up paying for it later. Stand up for yourself this afternoon, even if that means causing a stir. Your inner rebel has something to say.

Tuesday 15th

Look out for any conflict that may upset the balance and harmony you've been working on. You must be careful not to speak without thinking. You may wish to get your voice heard but pausing before reacting would be useful now. Tempers may be short and limits may be frustrating.

Wednesday 16th

The celestial lovers Mars and Venus meet under a full moon. You may see that your divine essence and childlike curiosity has played a big part in uniting your mental and emotional faculties. You may be under the spotlight in more ways than one. Shine your light brightly and it will attract others.

Thursday 17th

You could be very particular or fussy now. Perhaps you are finding a work issue frustrating and wish to try it your way. This may be acceptable if you can state your case clearly and thoroughly. Be open-minded and respectful and today you could be making super impressions on those who count.

Friday 18th

Your inner compass seems far away, but this doesn't stop you going after what you want. You may find something you never knew you wanted, and this suits you well. The Sun enters your career zone to open up your options. You could be satisfied with any small change today.

Saturday 19th

Today, romance and creativity are highlighted, and you may find that combined, they bring some harmony. You may wish to reconnect with friends from overseas who can teach you a few things about their world. Selfless causes touch you deeply and you may wish to offer your services.

Sunday 20th

It's possible that you feel a little off balance today. Maybe you are trying too hard to keep up the equilibrium you are enjoying. This is a passing phase and is nothing to worry about. Take a day of rest and allow yourself to have some alone time and indulge yourself.

Monday 21st

Ensure that you don't get taken advantage of today. Mars and Venus are still together but the energy is getting intense. You may find that you become resentful of time spent doing things for others. You may need to communicate this and let people know where your boundaries begin and end.

Tuesday 22nd

The day goes from tricky to easy and you must navigate the in-between. It may start with an urge to rebel against someone being possibly pushy or probing too deeply into your private life. By evening you may find your inner lover and know what to do to self-soothe and realign with your true north.

Wednesday 23rd

Thoughts of the past may fill your waking mind; you may have dreamed of someone you used to know. Old passions may flavour your day and you find letting it go easy. The past must stay where it is. This may give you an urge to explore more with your partner.

Thursday 24th

By chatting to people from distant lands, you may feel that your work life is limiting your prospects of travel. However, if you can be minded to, talk to your boss and you may find that it's quite the opposite and new avenues are opening for you.

Friday 25th

All is not lost. You may feel like you are swimming around an unknown ocean or clutching at straws. A lifejacket is needed to anchor you. Look at your relationships and your ability to work at projects from the bottom up. You have the dedication and determination to make anything work.

Saturday 26th

Practical work such as building, gardening or decluttering will be good for you today. You can also apply this to any inner work you may do, as this is also a clear-out of sorts. You may be pleasantly surprised or feel fresh and new. A load has been lifted from you.

Sunday 27th

Today is full of blessings, so be quick and catch them while you can. Your love life will benefit as will your work prospects. Mark this day as auspicious as it could be the start of something you've been wanting for a long time. Take it slowly and enjoy it.

Monday 28th

The past and future have a meeting point in the present. See if you can tune in to that energy today. You could be excitable and restless. Try not to rebel too much. Your heart and head are perfectly in sync and you may be feeling invincible.

MARCH
. . . .

Tuesday 1st

There may be a skill or talent you've used before that may come in use again now. Try digging around and recycling old ways. You may be able to come up with an ingenious solution to a problem at work. Set your mind to the task and you've an excellent chance at success.

Wednesday 2nd

A new moon can be the green light you've been waiting for regarding careers. Talking this over with a trusted elder or an overseas connection will improve your understanding. The great ideas keep flowing and your mind may be working overtime trying to process a lot of new stuff. Know your limits.

Thursday 3rd

This is a dreamy day where you may be romantically inclined to make big gestures. You could be considering how your love life and ambitions work together and are testing a partner's reactions. The planetary energy suggests that this is productive and positive. Maybe two heads are better than one now.

Friday 4th

Plan for some social time with friends. You may desire to let off steam or share your exciting news with others. If you're the one who normally rallies the troops then you can organise an event where you're centre of attention. Try hosting something different from the norm.

Saturday 5th

There is a golden opportunity today to make a great impression in the workplace. You are in the spotlight and people who matter are watching you. This is another chance to shine. Put your best foot forward and show people what you're made of. You may be positively assertive and outspoken.

Sunday 6th

The celestial lovers move into your travel zone together. This bodes well if you have committed to a trip, study or a wider world issue with your partner. You may need to take stock of this today. Make solid plans or at least set down the seeds for roots to grow.

Monday 7th

The clever ideas continue to flow from you. Today you may be more optimistic that things you are putting in place can help shift some outdated patterns of behaviour. There may be a clearing out of debris lurking in your psyche. Now is the right time to let it all go.

Tuesday 8th

You may face a small challenge regarding communication today. This may be a case of stubbornness and it's likely you who isn't budging. A swift change of perspective this evening helps you to be more flexible. Your mind is still full of inquiry but more willing to appease others.

Wednesday 9th

Today you have a rare moment where you may step outside your mind and observe yourself. Think about your views on other cultures. Is expanding your knowledge part of your true north? Might you have the opportunity for a working vacation doing something for the greater good?

Thursday 10th

Here is where serious networking begins. You may be more open to different viewpoints now. Be keen to learn what makes others tick and try merging your work with your personal interests. There is a lot to learn now and you may need to seek far and wide for answers.

Friday 11th

A weekend at home may be good for you. You could be feeling emotional or sentimental about your material goods and need the security of your home environment. This could be because you have a lot to think about and would prefer to do it from your safety zone.

Saturday 12th

Sensitive spots may be triggered but cause you no distress. In fact, you're likely to self-soothe and heal them now. Emotions may be bigger than usual, but this is fine. Perhaps you need to let stuff in and out to assess if they still hold value for you.

Sunday 13th

Today you can get a good look at your inner compass. It may be shining like a beacon with an obvious message for you. Jump aboard and head towards true north. It looks like a lot of things are lining up for you to begin the next phase of your personal journey.

Monday 14th

Try not to be too boisterous today when communicating. Your enthusiasm may not be shared by those you need to deal with. Don't run the risk of speaking your mind to someone who isn't prepared to listen as sadly this may trigger an old wound and cause you stress.

Tuesday 15th

There are still small challenges ahead today. You may need to retreat or call a truce on something. It's possible to get around the obstacles, but not alone. You might need a dedicated team to brainstorm with. Learning a new skill would come in handy as would reviving an old one.

Wednesday 16th

Chores at home may take up your time today. There is good energy for cleaning, decluttering and getting everything in order. Look at your daily routine and see if it includes time for you alone. You may be required to do jobs for others in your family. Do them with unconditional love.

Thursday 17th

It may be hard to express yourself. The trick is to let others know where your borders are and when you've had enough. You could be yearning to do your own thing but find that stirrings deep inside are keeping you in old habits of doing as you're told.

Friday 18th

There is a full moon, which may highlight any conflicts you've been having recently. Consider the balance of how much you do for others, and what you may receive in turn. Think about how you may change or transform this balance to benefit all.

Saturday 19th

If you're in the mood to open your heart, this can be a fruitful weekend. You may get a moment of doubt, which sets off an alarm bell in your psyche. Consider if this is something from the past you are repeating or if you're being overly cautious.

Sunday 20th

The Sun shifts into your social sector and heralds a time of high activity. Get out your planner and schedule events that are fun and vitalising. Try to ignore switching something up today as this may be an impulse that you will hate later. Your mood may turn inwards this afternoon.

Monday 21st

Your ruler, Mercury, may be filling your mind with lots of tasks and things to learn. You may be overwhelmed today, so take it easy. It's possible that you experience intense feelings of resentment over mundane duties that take you away from your path. Don't let this fester.

Tuesday 22nd

A sleepless night or one filled with strange dreams may leave you with some concerns. You may be reconnecting with an issue from the past that tugs on your heartstrings. By evening you may be anxious and irritable. Put your energy into something productive if this doesn't pass soon.

Wednesday 23rd

Relationships benefit from an uplifted mood. You could be more outgoing and optimistic now. Mercury visits your inner compass and you should be alert to any messages, whispers or signs in the workplace that you may wish to get on board with. Stay open-minded and teachable.

Thursday 24th

You may feel like running before you can walk today. If you do, you may come up against problems. Keep optimistic but also adaptable. Be willing to learn a lesson from someone you respect, as their wisdom and experience may benefit you in the long term. Keep romance respectful and take things slowly.

Friday 25th

Superficial will not do today. You may find that intentions within a group are not to your liking and you prefer to dig deeper. Your ego may take a bashing if you persist. However, this also triggers something deep inside, and you must learn to be humble amongst the collective.

Saturday 26th

If you are left alone, this can be a productive day on many levels. You have just the right energy to attempt large tasks but in small chunks. By evening you may have completed a project and feel satisfied with your day. Weekend working will reap the rewards you deserve.

Sunday 27th

You may be thinking about your role in the collective. A journey of discrimination within your personal social groups may be needed now. How do you contribute? Is there more you could do? Your curiosity and vision may see you in a leadership role, which could suit you very well.

Monday 28th

This is an important day to accept others. You may connect with people with differing viewpoints or cultural backgrounds. Whilst this can delight you, beware of becoming impatient if there's a language or communication barrier. Maintain harmony by being a good listener and showing compassion.

Tuesday 29th

Work is the theme of the day and not much else. You may be connecting to a large number of people and need to be flexible. You could also be run off your feet with chores that aren't your specialisms. Teamwork is necessary, so find your tribe and tackle this together.

Wednesday 30th

You could begin to see how all the small elements you've been working on attach to make a bigger picture now. Radical thinking may be required to solve a problem. By evening you may have more satisfaction from your work and can see that it aligns with your personal truth.

Thursday 31st

Change or eradication of something that isn't working is easy now. You may be making space for something new to come in and the disposal of the old has made that possible. Look ahead to what you can do now that you've cleared the decks. Fun weekend plans can be made.

APRIL
. . . .

Friday 1st
Your social life could be bursting with activity this month.
Perhaps you've imagined ways to host some get-togethers.
Today's new moon helps you to make plans that can be
vitalising. Inject a spark into your friendship groups and get
active. A leadership role could be waiting for you.

Saturday 2nd
Get outdoors today and enjoy spending time with like-minded
people. Shared passions can provide stimulating things to do.
You may also be connecting with overseas friends or interest
groups that strive to make the world a better place. Settle
down this evening and ruminate over new ideas until you fully
understand them.

Sunday 3rd
Your mental processes may feel slow after the recent high
activity. Your job is to feel into a new venture by listening and
observing. Mercury, your ruler needs you to be quiet and stay
alert for any messages or signposts. Release your inner genius
and think outside the box.

Monday 4th
It may be difficult to begin the working week. Your mind
may be elsewhere and not allowing you to focus. This can be
draining, so take a slow approach to your duties today. Do
nothing more than is essential. Your heart just isn't in it today,
so don't push it.

Tuesday 5th

An inner tension surfaces as you desire to get moving, but know that you have responsibilities that prevent this. Deep desires seem to evade you. However, you become more alert and curious as the day progresses. It just seems like you are waking up slowly and you don't like it.

Wednesday 6th

Today you may be far more bright and bubbly. Your typical Gemini attributes are on fire as your mind is stimulated by the tasks you are given. Your sponge-like curiosity is soaking everything up. Work your way through your 'to do' list and be proud of your achievements.

Thursday 7th

Stay sharp as you could be making a good impression on someone who matters. Networking and connecting with long-distance acquaintances can open up important channels for you now. Enjoy a sense of satisfaction at home with some luxury food or good company this evening. Treat yourself – you deserve it.

Friday 8th

Grab what is offered to you in the workplace today. This is a fortunate time, where your dreams and visions get a huge boost. This may be a cause for celebration as finances may get a lift too. Get your social groups together and have some fun. You could be networking like crazy now.

Saturday 9th

Your feelings of security could be at a more than comfortable level. However, don't overdo the good things in life and blow it all at once. Stay in your safety zone and put something aside for a rainy day. Your optimism and motivation to succeed are boundless today.

Sunday 10th

Don't be tempted to change or dismiss anything just yet. You could be rushing ahead of yourself and there may be a few more foundations you have to dig first. Nobody likes a show-off, so try to be more modest about your good fortune. Don't let your mouth run away with you.

Monday 11th

Mercury your ruler enters your most private area today. This may be a time when your inner critic, that little voice inside, fills you with doubt. Pay more attention to your inner cheerleader instead. Good luck continues to arrive. Ensure that it's really as good as it first looks.

Tuesday 12th

Heavy conversations may be exhausting but are necessary. You may be suspicious or feel undeserving of the good things you are being offered. Do your research, be meticulous and check all the facts. You could slip into negative thinking and miss your chance for success. Don't let this pass you by.

Wednesday 13th

Try not to self-sacrifice today. It could be that you dismiss your own needs or become too rigid. Get mundane duties out of the way and give yourself time to relax and unwind. You may have a breakthrough and get rid of old conditioning and habits.

Thursday 14th

A last-minute push may be needed to secure or complete a project with overseas connections. You may feel extra tired today as something weighs heavy on your mind. Make sure that you're not overthinking this. Let this phase pass and you will feel more balanced this evening.

Friday 15th

There are now four planets in your career sector, and you may find yourself overloaded with work duties. Use a filtering process and prioritise your tasks. If you need help, ask for it. Use someone as an anchor. Say afloat but be adaptable. Don't be a martyr and take on more than you can manage.

Saturday 16th

A full moon lights up your family zone and shows where there is balance and harmony, or not. This could also signal the success of a project where people have been working together to achieve something good. Relationships are also in focus now. Aim for equality and know your roles.

Sunday 17th

Emotions can be intense now and you may build a little resentment. Use this day to go with the flow and do basic tasks. You could be feeling driven to get to the bottom of an issue or learn more about topics that are deep and mysterious.

Monday 18th

Something from your past may come back to haunt you today. Your ruler is digging around in your psyche and has unearthed an issue that needs healing. Self-love is needed as you let this thing go forever. Later in the day, switch your focus to the good things happening in the workplace.

Tuesday 19th

Bring your important relationships into focus now and be guided by the support you have there. Your work may bring a challenge that you can't assimilate and use. Let it go and try another day with fresh eyes. Perhaps a partner can offer a solution or lift your mood.

Wednesday 20th

If you aren't careful you could be on a downward spiral. The sun enters your private zone and will show up your darkest corners. This is meant as a healing process, but you may be reluctant to do the work. Your career can be challenging today too. Don't give up on yourself.

Thursday 21st

A change of perspective lets you see your inner work as a challenge you wish to accept. You may resolve to take it slowly and use it as a chance to explore your depths. Once you have made up your mind, you can be thorough and will probably find you enjoy it.

Friday 22nd

You have a positive bounce to your work today. Others will be impressed and may join in your optimism. With this attitude, you can make a lot of headway at work and end the week well satisfied with your progress. You may notice that you are also on track and aligned.

Saturday 23rd

Friendship groups call for your presence this weekend. This may include online groups or study. Either way, you could be doing something that enriches your mind and lets you connect with like-minded people. You may discover a signpost that beckons you to a future goal you have been quietly harbouring.

79

Sunday 24th

Don't be too rigid in your thinking today. There is a lesson to be learned from an elder or person in authority and you need to have an open mind. This may clash with your old conditioning and you may need to evaluate both perspectives before accepting a new way.

Monday 25th

Being flexible at work may take you on a wild ride today, but you could enjoy it. You may find that you merge new ideas with old or have a newfound desire to get a few things straight. This may include your finances, investments or your bank balance in general.

Tuesday 26th

Today you are emotionally driven to get tasks done and cut away anything causing unnecessary blocks. You could come up with an innovative way of approaching a problem. If you are given time alone and work diligently, you may have your moment of genius. Everyone will benefit from this.

Wednesday 27th

This is a day full of blessings and good fortune. Watch how people will flock around you and share your light. As an auspicious day, a midweek celebration is in order and you could be hosting a get-together. Pause and notice how this is totally in line with your true north.

Thursday 28th

Keep your ears open as you may be given a new mission today. You can make changes and transformations like a magician now and others may marvel at how easily you do this. Deeply mysterious or underground topics may give you something new to delve into when you have time for research.

Friday 29th

Pluto turns retrograde today. Change is happening and your job is to lead the way for others to navigate it. You may have a sense of what your new mission is, but if you don't, go with the flow and all will become clear soon. Wait for a signal.

Saturday 30th

A new moon with a solar eclipse is your signal. This is a window of opportunity for you to dig deep in your personal resources and excavate the gold hidden in your psyche. Eclipses are wildcard energy, so keep an open mind. Mercury comes home to your sign today too.

MAY

. . . .

Sunday 1st

You may have a restlessness today. This is natural for a Gemini when there is something to aim for. The trick is knowing when is the time to act. There isn't much you can do at the moment, so put that energy into something else. Make a vision board and spend time visualising your dreams.

Monday 2nd

Optimism fuels your day. You have big ideas and even bigger dreams, which you can now begin to implement. The Moon meets your ruler in your sign; take this emotional attachment to your new mission and start to connect with the right people. Reach out to your social groups.

Tuesday 3rd

Get all the busy stuff done early as you may run out of steam this afternoon. Try not to give yourself too much choice now as you could be overwhelmed and doubt yourself again. Tackle one thing at a time and rest when you need to. Let your mind filter everything new.

Wednesday 4th

Your mental energy may be lively but can still drain you. Nothing is impossible, but you must remember that there are times when too much can make you vaguer and more indecisive. You could have some success by working on deeper personal issues instead.

Thursday 5th

Set up camp in your home for the next day or two. You may be feeling vulnerable and not wish to expose too much of what is going on for you. Get some nourishing food and good company around. You could experience bursts of enlightenment from your psyche. Clarity lights up dark corners.

Friday 6th

Friends and acquaintances can be supportive and informative today. It's worth hanging out with people who have the experiences you are wishing for. A money-making scheme could be one of the things your social groups encourage you to do now. Be thankful for the right connections you have.

Saturday 7th

Don't let anyone tell you how to do your own work. Long-distance communications may cause a small problem. You may need to attend to an urgent work issue before taking the next steps. Make sure you have some fun this evening and let your hair down. Shine your light for others.

Sunday 8th

Getting together with your soul group would be good today. Take a day of letting your tribe know how much you value their presence in your life. Be an inspiration to them and you may find that they offer you the same. Have an hour or two to yourself this evening.

Monday 9th

You may encounter a few challenges that don't sit right with you. Don't make too much of this as it's a passing phase. If you feel limited or unable to express yourself, let it go. Try again another day with fresh eyes. There's no point giving yourself unnecessary stress.

Tuesday 10th

Your ruler Mercury turns retrograde today in your sign. This will be a few weeks where you revise your outlook or go deep into a new project you've been assigned. Try not to make any commitments just yet. Double-check travel plans and ensure communications are crystal clear. Check everything twice.

Wednesday 11th

Jupiter moves into your friendship zone, so prepare for a boost in activity here. However, use your energy wisely today as work may come with a heavy load and make you feel drained. Your family life may also tire you. Try to switch off this evening and do something that requires no effort.

Thursday 12th

Get creative today. Romance may have been lacking lately, so do something about it. Check in or reconnect with someone and explore ideas for meet-ups that suit you both. You could be called on to mediate or settle a dispute. Now is not the time to waiver or be indecisive.

Friday 13th

You may have a moment where private issues are exposed for your own good. It could be that you've been dragging your feet or refusing to adapt to something, and you now have a change of heart. Be glad that is no longer holding back your progress.

Saturday 14th

Remember that everyone has boundaries and they may not be the same as yours. Pushing other people's buttons won't achieve the changes you require in an intimate relationship. Content yourself with doing weekend chores and make time for pleasure this evening. Share intense feelings with someone you trust implicitly.

Sunday 15th

It's possible that you have triggered something deep within you. However, this may not be a bad thing. Perhaps you are realising your true feelings run deeper than you previously thought. Partner time can be sensual, and you may find that your relationship goes up to a level that excites you.

Monday 16th

A full moon and lunar eclipse close the wildcard window. This may also seal a deal you have made with a partner. It can also show where you need to take more care of your health. Romance is still on the agenda if you can keep it unconditional.

Tuesday 17th

Outgoing energy can make you a fireball today. You may be bouncing around full of positive energy and everyone wants a piece. Share your optimism and joy with those around you and you will be rewarded with the same. This is a great day for brainstorming with groups and lovers.

Wednesday 18th

You could be rushed off your feet today. The planetary energy also suggests that you are moving towards your dreams and ambitions and putting a great deal of effort into them. Try taking things a little slower as you may miss out on important details and will have to backtrack.

Thursday 19th

Solid, practical work will keep you busy but may also prove challenging. You may need to investigate something deeply. However, this is good for you as it keeps you on task. It may also prove beneficial to a personal issue and helps you deal with that too. Just be gentle with yourself.

Friday 20th

You are a workhorse today. It is noticed that you are working diligently and getting good results. Just be careful not to get ahead of yourself and make silly mistakes. Be mindful of your conversations and be respectful when networking. Remember Mercury is retrograde, so filter your language before speaking.

Saturday 21st

The Sun has entered your sign. Happy birthday! You could have a couple of challenges this evening and your ruler is involved. Stay away from gossip and keep a low profile. A day of reading or researching would be a good activity and will keep you out of trouble.

Sunday 22nd

You would do well to listen to the advice of elders in your interest groups. It could be you who is called upon to voice an opinion. If you must, make it kind, respectful and honest. It would be better if you declined if you feel too emotionally involved.

Monday 23rd

This is a day to finish loose ends at work. You may notice that your mental processes appear to be alight with ideas and you have many things going on at once. Focus on the one that will bring you more gain and you will succeed.

Tuesday 24th

Your inner compass is within your grasp. You may reach for it with far more enthusiasm than of late. Just wait until Mercury retrograde is over and you can make a start. Hold your big plans for now. There may be more to excavate in your psyche that will enhance your personal growth.

Wednesday 25th

Social interactions or things you do for the greater good are particularly favoured now. It's possible that you've joined a cause and are fighting for the rights of a collective. You will have extra energy for this now that Mars is here. Use your inquisitive nature to inspire others.

Thursday 26th

You could get a lot of emotional satisfaction from your interest groups today. It seems that everyone knows their roles and duties and things tick along nicely. Limits and boundaries are respected. Ideas can flow when all are singing from the same page. Keep leading and inspiring your groups to action.

Friday 27th

Control issues or power struggles may surface today. You may need to get to the bottom of this before attempting to make progress. Keep emotions out of it as you could easily be dragged in. Stay logical, rational and fair. Use your powers to mediate the situation and avoid tension.

Saturday 28th

A day of rest may be needed. You may need to let off steam in private or with trusted friends. Meditation or a yoga practice would be good. Venus enters your most personal zone to help you recognise the beauty in your shadow. Self-care will become more important now.

Sunday 29th

High activity within your social groups may drag you out of hiding. There could be a conflict that gets out of hand. You may have trouble reconciling some things as your emotions are turned inwards and you could feel powerless. Wait until this evening when you may think more clearly.

Monday 30th

A new moon in your sign is another green light. Set goals and intentions around you and only you. If there is something you wish to change about your appearance, outlook or the way you are perceived, do it now. A new course of study would also be good for you now.

Tuesday 31st

Your mind may be clear and fresh today. It could also be hungry for new stimulation and mental challenge. You may find what you're looking for by evening, but it may also jar with your true north. Perhaps a change of perspective is needed before rushing into this.

JUNE
....

Wednesday 1st

It's fine to withdraw from company and look after your own needs today. In your social groups, you may see some aggression or activity that is exhausting. Take care of yourself by protecting your energy and enjoying the safety of your own home, maternal company and your favourite foods.

Thursday 2nd

Staying in your safety bubble may stir something in your psyche. This could be an urge to break free whilst being nurtured by your family. It may be that you rebel against tradition and go your own way. This could be a simple as changing a family favourite recipe to suit yourself.

Friday 3rd

Mercury turns direct now. Go over old ground and get absolutely certain that what you want is right for you. Your inner voice will signal if it is. As you crawl out of your shell the world may not look so frightening, but the rest has recharged and revitalised you.

Saturday 4th

Saturn turns retrograde now. As the biggest teacher of the planets, you will be tested on boundaries and limitations. You may begin by looking at your social groups and what your role might be. A rebellion of sorts may be brewing, and you may need to take on more responsibilities.

Sunday 5th

If you want your say today, it comes with a risk. You may step out of line and cross someone important. This may also play on your mind and peel back a layer of tension that reveals old wounds and similar situations. Old coping mechanisms won't work anymore.

Monday 6th

Your mind may be doing overtime and conflicting with your need to express yourself. Think before reacting, pause before responding and try not to use your words as weapons. This is a day to learn some humility and look at your own actions. You may need to unlearn bad habits.

Tuesday 7th

Practical activity will bring you back to a state of inner peace. You may be wondering how to shift the patterns of behaviour that are letting you down. Do some quiet digging around in your psyche and you may find that self-care and physical exercise can calm that overactive mind of yours.

Wednesday 8th

Give yourself time to declutter something now. This could be from something inside you that needs disposing of once and for all. There are some things that aren't working for you, such as conditioned behaviours learned as a child. Dig deep and let go of these, but do it slowly.

Thursday 9th

You may have a conflict between your love life and your obligations with friends. Spending quality time on creative and romantic pursuits will bring you more joy than being active with social groups. A balance of both is ideal but if that drains you, stick to what is more personal.

Friday 10th

A boundary may present you with a challenge today. Try not to control the situation and you may find that it works out better. A little voice inside may tell you that it's okay to grieve a loss or change, but not to dwell on it too much.

Saturday 11th

You could be particularly stubborn and refuse to go along with the crowd. A day of self-care of doing something sensual would be good. You may also have time to think about money-making schemes or brand-new ways of relating. Your inner child may be wanting to get out and play.

Sunday 12th

Intense feelings may bubble up and need your attention. You could be thinking about old love affairs that have left a mark on you. Don't spend your energy on past events. Nostalgia doesn't hurt unless it touches a wound you haven't healed yet. Let your head, not your heart guide you.

Monday 13th

A total flip of reason may occur today. Your current personal relationships draw you closer and your mind comes back to the present. Mercury has come back to your sign and makes you think more wisely. Your passion and desire to help others within a social setting also returns.

Tuesday 14th

A full moon in your relationship sector shows how far you've come and how far you still wish to go. Nothing can stop you now and this energy may allow you to reach further than before. You may also see the fruition of a project involving travel or other cultures.

91

Wednesday 15th

Lie low today as you could be attempting to climb a mountain without a guide. You may also be feeling intense emotions surrounding friendship groups or joint ventures. Stay in a safety bubble and let this pass as it could overwhelm you and drain all your energy if you're not careful.

Thursday 16th

Use baby steps today and be very gentle with yourself. Earthy energy suggests that you need more grounding and would do well to take care of your own needs or do something that has solid results. Get rid of unnecessary stress and lighten your load by sticking to your limits.

Friday 17th

You may wish to connect with others and party. It's impossible to keep you down for long – you thrive on connection. Get your leader hat on and revive your role within your social groups. They may be waiting for your next brilliant idea.

Saturday 18th

Try not to get frustrated today. You may be pushing boundaries, and this is exactly what you shouldn't do. If you feel stuck, stop and reflect. Maybe this is a no-go area for you, and you should re-evaluate a few things. It may not be in your best interests to persevere.

Sunday 19th

Give yourself a good talking to now. Your inner compass wants you to merge with what is in alignment with you. That must come from deep inside you and must begin with self-love. Your head and heart are not in sync. As a Geminian, you must listen to your head.

Monday 20th

It may feel that you've missed out on something today. This is the influence of the Sun about to leave your sign. Think of it as your awareness being triggered, and now you have the chance to assimilate what you've learned. Your true north is in sight this evening.

Tuesday 21st

The summer solstice arrives. The longest day lets you scan around you and ensure you're still on track. Social groups are optimistic and motivated by recent changes, and could be on your schedule for a celebration this evening. Get your thinking cap on and aim to impress or encourage others.

Wednesday 22nd

Today may be emotionally draining as you could be overworked or taking too much on. It could also be a day where you power through and get a lot done. A midweek event with friends may keep you going but can also be the source of extreme tiredness by evening. Take it easy.

Thursday 23rd

Venus enters your sign, so if your self-care routine has been lacking, it may improve now. You could start winding down for the weekend a little early and choose to have some quality time alone or get loved up with a special someone. You deserve some pleasure and light relief.

Friday 24th

What is brewing in your most private thoughts? An emotional flashback could lead to an outburst or a disturbance you'd rather not deal with. This energy may also signify that you are deeply moved by a connection and the earth shakes under your feet. What is rocking your world?

Saturday 25th

You may have a glimpse of the future now. Are you still on the right path? Check in with your true north and if you have been straying, you can pull yourself back in line. There is still a mountain to climb, but there's no need to rush.

Sunday 26th

Spend today doing something that makes you feel fully alive. Romance is highlighted, as is self-care and attending to your own needs. If there is something new you'd like to do, today's energy can help give you the motivation you need. This can expand your horizons.

Monday 27th

You have a busy head and heart today. Listen to your inner critic but pay more attention to your inner cheerleader and allow yourself some praise. You may find that friendship groups require you to step out of your comfort zone and this may cause you to evaluate their worth.

Tuesday 28th

Neptune turns retrograde today. As this is the planet signifying your inner compass, you may feel a little lost for a while. This gives you the chance to go over everything you've learned, try different things and decide if you're still happy with them in your life.

Wednesday 29th

If things seem a little much today, stay where you are nurtured and loved. A new moon suggests that a few things need to change. How do you nourish your soul? Is your immediate environment supporting or smothering? Check in with your maternal line and feed from their intuition and wisdom.

Thursday 30th

Quality is important to you now and you may think about what needs switching up and refreshing. A home makeover or a personal image change may revitalise you. Start looking at things from a different perspective and evaluate what they are worth to you. Material things may hold less importance now.

JULY

. . . .

Friday 1st

Be bold and brave. Say what you wish to say, even if it sounds wacky or irrational. A grievance spoken aloud can be solved or at least soothed. Friends and social groups can be supportive, so plan some time with people you trust and care for.

Saturday 2nd

Try not to overstep the mark now, as your communications may be innocent to you but pushy to another. You could be frustrated by this and wish you hadn't spoken in the first place. Pull your energy back in and explore your conversational habits. Are they preventing you from making real connections?

Sunday 3rd

Don't be afraid to get back out into the world today. You have much to learn and may have a lot of questions. Slow down and make yourself as clear as you can. Family time this afternoon can help you to sort through a few troublesome issues.

Monday 4th

You may have an urge to complete a project with your social groups today. Maybe one last push will finalise an important step towards presenting a concept to others. If you sense that you are doing more than your fair share, speak up and ask for help. Don't be a scapegoat.

Tuesday 5th

It's time to learn how to gather your resources and ensure that your immediate environment is filled with things you love. You may put more effort into laying solid foundations or securing finances, thereby creating a comfortable zone to enjoy. Look at healthy eating and plan some great meals.

Wednesday 6th

You could be looking at ways of romancing a special someone or entertaining in your home. However, things may not go to plan and your mood may become grumpy. You don't have to provide anything spectacular. Aim for a well-balanced event with mutual respect, good conversation and shared interests.

Thursday 7th

Use your mental faculties with compassion today. You may be asked to mediate or comment on something that needs your particular expertise. Think before responding and use kindness if you must be critical. You can do this without hurting anyone's feelings. Your status may go up a notch if you can manage this.

Friday 8th

Check in with your health and take things easy as today could drain your energy. You could be starting on the next phase of a project and will need a lot of concentration. Use your capacity to soak up knowledge but refrain from taking on duties that aren't yours.

Saturday 9th

You may have a lot of restless energy and desire to do something radical this weekend. Think twice if this involves spending resources you don't have. Superficiality doesn't satisfy you today and you may be rebellious or think outside the box for something deep and mysterious to occupy you.

Sunday 10th

Get a partner on board with your unusual ideas today. They may encourage you to expand your horizons even more. Try not to stay in your safety zone where there is no room for growth. Find your edge and push it a little further. Be brave and change an old habit.

Monday 11th

Second-guessing yourself won't help today. All you need is alone time this evening to recharge your batteries. Online friends can provide inspiration and feed your soul with positivity. It may be that you feel unworthy of a position and doubt your abilities. Let you friends be your cheerleaders now.

Tuesday 12th

You may settle into the working week a little late but when you do, you work hard and are productive. Today you may see more progress than usual as your focus could be on attaining a specific goal. You could be taking work home or attempting your personal challenges this evening.

Wednesday 13th

A full moon can show you the summit or a great achievement today. You may feel the build-up to it as agitation or possibly fear. Know that you are fully supported and people around you just want to see and share in your success. There may be a celebration too.

Thursday 14th

Your mind may feel like a lot of fireworks going off at once and you're not sure how you feel about it. The energy is positive, but you may doubt yourself or be a little suspicious. It could activate something deep inside you that is asking to break free.

Friday 15th

The urge to rebel or do something outside the box may be overwhelming today. You could be having conversations that make you rethink a lot of what you believe. This may be uncomfortable, but you enjoy the mental challenge. Think everything through before acting or making a final commitment to this.

Saturday 16th

This is a lovely day for connecting or merging with your higher self. You may be more inclined to do what makes you feel good. Take in more information than you give out today. Listening to your inner voice can help to realign you with your goal. A quest may be revealed.

Sunday 17th

Dig deep within and pull out something that you've been hiding for some time. It may be time to shake up an old habit or treat yourself to a longstanding desire. Don't think too much about it or you may miss your chance. Loving words are waiting to be spoken.

Monday 18th

Your sense of safety and security, particularly regarding money, may be enhanced now. There could be changes from which you will benefit financially in the long-term. You may have ideas that at first feel strange, but you will soon grow accustomed to them. Find what suits you and your circumstances best.

Tuesday 19th

It's time to step out of your safety zone if you wish to grow. Conversations and networking with others may bring out the best in you. The information you seek may become available to you, so be ready to take it all in.

Wednesday 20th

You may struggle with a few things today as you adjust to a new way of being. You could feel extra protective of your resources until you accept that change is inevitable and necessary for your growth. Look within this evening and seek out what you need to let go of.

Thursday 21st

Your head and heart may not feel in sync today; follow your heart. It will show you what you need to feel worthy and can give you the push you need. This afternoon you can be more driven to doing your inner work and letting yourself shine in the world.

Friday 22nd

Unsettled energy can be annoying as you see the path ahead but also notice the roadblocks. Knowledge is the key now; use all the information you have and look for avenues that can help you apply it. Break down old walls and personal boundaries as these are the restrictions you are seeing.

Saturday 23rd

The Moon in your sign gives you more confidence in your convictions. You may resolve to do what is necessary and take a courageous stand. There may be no stopping you now as you articulate your needs easily. Be careful as you may be unfiltered and shock people.

Sunday 24th

Your ego may be inflated today, and you could feel self-righteous about issues you find important. Make sure that you don't preach to the converted. Your social and interest groups may be encouraging but could also give you false confidence that needs to be tempered with a sense of responsibility.

Monday 25th

It's possible that you clash with groups and realise that they aren't in your best interests after all. If in doubt, stick with what makes you feel safe and protected. You may wish to retreat and assess things in private. Female relatives or maternal figures can be nurturing and supportive.

Tuesday 26th

Take time to gather your thoughts and stay in your comfort zone if you need to. You may be regretting coming out of it. Don't worry about what others think. This could be a small hiccup where you realise the need to slow down. Self-care is essential to your wellbeing.

Wednesday 27th

You may be more determined to do some inner work and excavate areas of your behaviour that are holding you back. Go easy on yourself. An old wound may be waiting to be healed. You may also have a change of heart or perspective that helps you be more accepting.

Thursday 28th

A new moon lets you set new intentions regarding how you communicate, play, laugh and express yourself. This could be advantageous and will help you evolve. However, Jupiter turns retrograde and you may have a period of slowing down and turning inwards, learning and absorbing these lessons fully before applying them.

Friday 29th

You could be feeling stubborn today and refusing to change anything. Resisting necessary change won't help you grow. This is a passing phase where you may just need time to play or relax before getting back into the hard work. Just do something light-hearted and unwind this weekend.

Saturday 30th

Your head and heart are in sync today. Playtime, romance or creative efforts would be good. There is no need to do anything heavy or serious as this will take away your fun. Be open to serving others and being helpful. You could get more satisfaction from doing mundane duties now.

Sunday 31st

Conversations can be a struggle as you may wish to know more than you are privy to. Try not to push boundaries or come across as a know-it-all. You may need to revise your communication skills when dealing with someone in authority. Probing won't do you any favours.

AUGUST

·················

Monday 1st

Volatile energy may propel you into the future by revealing something from your past that you've kept hidden. Family members are on hand for emotional support and may help you get rid of something that no longer serves you. This could be a belief about yourself that has been wrong.

Tuesday 2nd

The disruption in your psyche may leave you feeling unsteady. Re-evaluate your self-worth and give your inner child the love and acknowledgement it craves. Balancing time with romantic partners and friends may be difficult as you are more sensitive to disharmony now and wish to do right by everyone.

Wednesday 3rd

Make your voice heard today. You may wish to settle a dispute in your love life or get creative and speak out through your art. Emotions may be strained as once again your inquisitive mind needs to know more information. If it isn't available to you, don't push it and get yourself frustrated.

Thursday 4th

Look to your family for the answers you seek. Mercury enters this sector and can help you to sort through intense feelings methodically. Be rational but go as deep as you are comfortable with. You may need to have difficult discussions now and disrupt the status quo.

Friday 5th

Today you have an opportunity to look at past karma and how it still affects you. A trigger may take you to a deeper understanding of some core issues you have been struggling with. Finances and shared ventures may be the theme here. What was once covered up will now be revealed.

Saturday 6th

You may be emotionally intense today, but this is all part of the healing process. Try not to discard everything that comes up for you. Some of it may teach you a valuable lesson about yourself. Take extra time today and be good to yourself. Be with those who nourish and nurture you.

Sunday 7th

A romantic partner may be your best ally now. If you aren't getting as much support from family as you'd like, look to your lover who can do their best to soothe you and remind you of your worth. A yearning to get back on track with your inner compass may fill you.

Monday 8th

Try to see things through a different set of eyes today. It may be useful to refresh your boundaries with others or at least remind them of where the line is. Things may look blurred right now and you need clarity. A practical activity can help you this evening.

Tuesday 9th

Look at your resources, especially those where you are tied to another. Joint financial ventures may feel the strain today. Apply the facts to what you already know and see if you can sift through anything that is outstanding, overdue or no longer needed. Old subscriptions may be cancelled.

Wednesday 10th

Digging deep is possibly the way to go today. There may be a lot of excavating to do but this can help you get rid of what is causing stress. You need to be in control of finances and your quality of life, or it may consume you. Revolt if necessary.

Thursday 11th

You could be feeling rebellious and take a stand today. When your emotions have calmed down, you can tackle any communication problems with more harmony. Try adopting the guise of the compassionate warrior and fighting your battles fairly and using words that can persuade rather than offend others.

Friday 12th

You may have several challenges today that can trigger negative emotions for you. A full moon throws a spotlight on your distant connections and travel opportunities. You may find that plans from earlier in the year have come to fruition and there is a chance for you to do something real for the greater good.

Saturday 13th

Show what you're made of now. Stand up for your own rights and those of others. You could be fighting a cause or demonstrating the art of rhetoric. Today, however, you are more likely to be speaking up for the underdog and putting your personal speeches to one side.

Sunday 14th

A great feeling of connection with the wider world keeps you going today. You are highly driven to do the right thing and make lasting changes. This could be in line with your true north. Keep doing it. Celebrate with a group this evening.

Monday 15th

You have a keen sense of justice today and may not take kindly to wrongdoings amongst your social groups. Speaking to family members can help you make sense of a few things from within your psyche. You could start delegating some of your mundane duties and freeing up your time.

Tuesday 16th

Know your limits today and all will be well. If you find a restriction, honour it and don't push through. Everything is in motion and you are enjoying the momentum. A small setback can be worked around and not prevent your progress. You could have an 'aha' moment with family.

Wednesday 17th

Drop down into yourself today and try to unwind. You may find this difficult as you are uplifted and need to continue your good work. Don't feel guilty about taking time for yourself. You need to recharge too. Allow yourself some pleasure and luxury time with good food and company.

Thursday 18th

It is important to break free from perceived restraints and free your mind today. Tie up a loose end before marching onwards and claiming space for yourself. Practical chores such as gardening, or meditative yoga would be good to clear your mind and get grounded. Ensure your roots are strong.

Friday 19th

Get ready to put into practice all you've been working on recently. You may have a change of mind about something you once felt affiliated to. Gather your resources and prepare to climb another mountain on your journey of self-development.

Saturday 20th

The Moon and Mars both enter your sign today and you are emotionally driven to work hard on something new. You may need to wait a short while, but you have the right motivation now and are willing to walk your talk. Let people see that you are determined to make a difference in the wider world and your own life.

Sunday 21st

You may wish to take stock of a few things. It could be necessary to sit with family and revise daily schedules so that no-one is doing more than their fair share. If everyone has a chance to speak, you may get a better idea of how things are working, or not.

Monday 22nd

Draw together all your resources and look at what is sustaining you and what is a waste of time. You may be able to add more value and quality just by losing something that no longer brings you joy. Think about what you need and what you want.

Tuesday 23rd

As the Sun enters your family sector, you could see more teamwork and sharing of tasks. You may also feel better in yourself as your health could be picking up now. Shared ventures or interests are highlighted today, and these may be the topic of conversation for a while.

Wednesday 24th

Uranus turns retrograde today. You may notice that issues from your psyche that were raised earlier this year will now be put to the test. For now, deal with what is good around you and take control of your immediate environment. Your money and home need to be your safety zones.

Thursday 25th

If today is a little tense and nothing is going your way, use it as a chance to pause and reflect. Progress is not stopped, but you have an opportunity to stand in the centre and assess how far you've come so far. Be an observer today.

Friday 26th

You may be in a unique position today that requires you to be extra compassionate and fair. It's possible that you are standing between two roadblocks. One involves your personal truths and rebellious nature, whilst the other requires you to conform and not rock the boat. Don't make an ill-informed decision.

Saturday 27th

A new moon in your family zone allows you to set down new rules and schedules for all. This may be long overdue but will relieve the pressure from some members who may be struggling. You may need to make a small sacrifice or put extra effort into making this work.

Sunday 28th

You are ready to shake things up today. The compassionate warrior side of you may be ready to speak out for the collective, but you could be opposed and lose interest. A small act of kindness or a word to the right people will employ this energy in a positive direction.

Monday 29th

Your mind and heart are in perfect harmony today. Attempts to reconcile with a lover or create something beautiful have a strong chance at success. You are driven to mediate and achieve a good balance of masculine and feminine energy. Thinking logically and using your emotions can bring you the results you desire.

Tuesday 30th

There may be a struggle today as you could clash with a person in authority or from your social circles. This can be blown over quickly if you stay respectful and fair. Otherwise, it could be exaggerated and lead to something distasteful. Honesty and leadership skills are needed now.

Wednesday 31st

Intense feelings may bring control issues to the fore within your social groups. If you see passive-aggressive behaviour, it is best to stay out of it. If you must try negotiating, be aware that the other person may not be ready to listen, and you could be fighting a losing battle.

SEPTEMBER
·················

Thursday 1st

Thoughts of the past could drag you into nostalgia. Take care
that this isn't idealistic thinking. You may yearn to be back
in better times, but you could also have karma to deal with.
Perhaps a score needs to be settled or something should be let
go to lighten your load.

Friday 2nd

You could be feeling sad or depressed today as triggers deep in
your psyche come up to be healed. You may need to go with
the flow as pushing against the tide will be futile. Go within
and discover what needs to be discarded or transformed.

Saturday 3rd

Partner time is on the agenda. Deep discussions may be lively,
and you have a chance to get a lot off your mind. You may wish
to resist the feelings this brings up as they rub against your
sense of security. Share only what you feel is safe and don't
compromise your self-worth.

Sunday 4th

Boundaries are in place to keep you from straying and getting
hurt. Speak your truth without getting aggressive. It may feel
that your inner compass is nowhere to be found right now but
this is a passing phase and you should look at other options
that suit you.

Monday 5th

You will get a lot more done if you resist pushing other people's buttons. Friendship groups may not give you the support you desire, and it may be hard to communicate or create today. Keep your thoughts to yourself for now or speak to those in your family who you can trust.

Tuesday 6th

Your productivity may be better today as you are more accepting of a challenge. If you can understand that everything has a beginning, and certain steps to follow, you may stay motivated. Keep your mind on the job or do other practical tasks to stay grounded. Be open-minded about change.

Wednesday 7th

Today has more air energy for you to access and be your best self. Problem-solving may occupy you and you could have some success if you think outside the box. Your excellent communication skills and natural curiosity can energise you and reap rewards. Social groups value your opinions.

Thursday 8th

Breaking free from traditional thinking may seem like an answer to some problems but you may need to confirm this with a person in authority. This could feel limiting and annoying to you but will give you a chance to look at angles you may not have previously considered.

Friday 9th

You could be much more willing to merge with the collective and be adaptable today. Work or spiritual groups may entice you out of your safety zone. Go with it as this is growth. Find your own edge and soften it a little. This could be scary at first but try it.

Saturday 10th

A busy day brings a full moon and Mercury retrograde. Together they can make you romantic or creative. However, take care this retrograde as it will mostly affect your love life and will be a balancing act. Back up devices and be very clear when communicating or relating to others.

Sunday 11th

This may be a good time to connect with others in order to brainstorm a few ideas. If you can accept that other opinions matter, you'll make big waves today and could come up with something truly innovative and unique. However, your ruler Mercury may make it difficult for you to agree with the majority today.

Monday 12th

You could be itching to take an active role today. It would be better if you could accept that traditional roles aren't working and devise a better format. Put your busy mind into group ventures, travel opportunities or researching other cultures and their values.

Tuesday 13th

If you have trouble convincing others to come on board with your schemes, don't get pushy. Take time to go within and consider if these have solid enough foundations. It could be that your own inner stubbornness is at fault here and it needs shaking up. Old habits may die hard today.

Wednesday 14th

Be kind to yourself and look to the future. This may involve digging around in your psyche for the golden nuggets that you hide away. Extract these and show them the light. Family members can be supportive and encourage you to be your best self for all to see.

Thursday 15th

Get physical or apply yourself to practical tasks today. Spend time looking at your inner compass and assessing what may need revising. You may need to look at another perspective and see if you've been too idealistic. Stay true to your essence and try not to waiver if there are disappointments.

Friday 16th

Your mind is racing today, and you may have no time for fools or antagonists. You should be able to see your true north today and have more of an understanding of what isn't attainable. Look through the mist that is hiding things you cling onto but that no longer serve you.

Saturday 17th

As a rule, assertiveness may not be your strong point, but today you are driven to prove that wrong. This may cause tension in your family group and throw you a few obstacles. If it's your own limits and boundaries you are asserting, this is good, just don't impose them on others.

Sunday 18th

A short retreat from the outside world will do you good. Perhaps take a duvet day and get cosy with your favourite snacks and movies. You may feel extra defensive of your space and reluctant to share your time and energy with a lover or friend.

Monday 19th

Grounding energy helps to settle you into the week; however, you may still need to isolate and stay in your comfort zone this evening. Let yourself be nourished and nurtured by your environment or close family. A detox from some areas of life may be needed in order to recharge.

Tuesday 20th

Freeing yourself from unnecessary duties and making time for yourself can help you get a fresh perspective. You may feel less defensive and ready to come out of your hidey-hole. Surprise yourself by showing up and making contact with relatives or long-lost friends. Late night conversations are on the agenda.

Wednesday 21st

Be incredibly careful today as you may be outspoken to the wrong groups and get into trouble. Due to Mercury, you may find yourself in a tricky situation or two that will be difficult to back out of. Remind yourself not to speak out unless it is honest, kind and respectful.

Thursday 22nd

More tripwires are waiting for you today. You could be fired up and ready to make progress and, with that momentum, find you fall right into them. One may be an old habit or behaviour that you default to when stressed. Another could be your impatience and failure to heed advice. Take things steady.

Friday 23rd

Mercury is in the heart of the Sun and is asking you to listen and receive new downloads. Open yourself up as a channel today. This could be an auspicious time for creative and romantic projects, but you will need to ensure you hear the message loud and clear.

Saturday 24th

You may feel drained today and like to switch off and be alone. Think about your own needs for once. If you are happy to be of service to others, make sure they don't take advantage. Challenge yourself to find a new way of unwinding this evening. It could be fun.

Sunday 25th

A family day may be enjoyable if your heart is in it. However, remember that Mercury may influence the conversation. A new moon may spark the attention of your muse and get your creative and romantic juices flowing. Lovers can pledge allegiances and deepen their understanding of each other.

Monday 26th

You may not have any time for social groups now, as your love life is foremost in your mind. Mind what you say now because if it isn't heartfelt, it will come back to haunt you later on. Egos may be over-inflated, so watch out for self-important behaviours.

Tuesday 27th

You could be trying too hard to maintain a nice balance between doing things for yourself and showing up for others. Step back and see that it comes naturally today. Pay more attention to any crisis or difficulty within your family. There may be a forced ending or change to deal with.

Wednesday 28th

Today you have an opportunity to re-establish your own boundaries. Let people know how much you are willing to do for them unconditionally but also show them your limits. This could provoke intense feelings and you may wish to investigate where these have come from.

Thursday 29th

Today may be tricky as you navigate between old patterns, karma and boundaries. Nothing is clear at the moment, so don't push for a signpost as you may still go the wrong way. Your love life may pick up pace now that Venus has made her home here for a few weeks.

Friday 30th

Partner time is highlighted and can bring emotions that are as deep as they are wide. You may be carried away on a tide of euphoria or whisked off on a weekend get-away. Romance is the only thing on your mind today and you may be showered with good fortune and happy moments.

OCTOBER
· ·

Saturday 1st

Reach out for something new and expansive today. Broaden your mind but remember your limits. It's possible that you push too far and cross a boundary, causing some upset this evening. You may also be required by family and friends, but could be reluctant to tear yourself away from a partner.

Sunday 2nd

Mercury turns direct and you may realise that you have been looking at something the wrong way. Your inner compass can guide you, but you will need to do the groundwork yourself. Go over recent events and see what still attracts and holds value for you.

Monday 3rd

Ease yourself into the week by taking small steps in your tasks. It would be helpful to bring out your inner genius and look for better ways of approaching problems. A breakthrough may happen when you break free from traditional ways of working and you could be credited for that.

Tuesday 4th

An outgoing mood and a busy mind mean that connecting and networking with others is important to you. You have the advantage today as good energy breathes fresh air into old relating patterns. You may earn something that attracts you to do more for the wider world and your partnerships.

Wednesday 5th

Feeling stuck is an invitation to pause and reflect. You appear to be learning a lot right now, but this will need practical application too. A teacher or respected friend may show you how to do something, from which you can learn more about self-discipline and when to act.

Thursday 6th

Impress people with your flexibility and show off your strengths, one of which is adapting well to new things. Going with the flow comes easily today and you may feel light and optimistic. Your creative side may merge with your work duties today.

Friday 7th

If there's a project that needs doing before the weekend, spend your energy today on that. This may involve a family issue or a thorough clean-up or discarding of something that is now obsolete. Make space and lighten your duties ready for fresh, new opportunities to come in and inspire you to grow.

Saturday 8th

You could be feeling tired and will feel like you are being lazy. Take a day off and play around with your inner compass. Be prepared to listen to opinions, even if they aren't helpful or informed. A social activity could be fun and be the push you need to drag you out of a slump.

Sunday 9th

Pluto turns direct and continues through your intimacy sector asking you to get deep and meaningful with people you value. A full moon shows the completion of a project with your social groups but can also expose those who aren't pulling their weight. Share duties in a combined cause.

Monday 10th

The day begins with great energy to keep you motivated and on task. However, you may need to use more practical than mental skills this afternoon as a new task could require a game plan that will be slow for you. Keep it attainable and don't rush into it.

Tuesday 11th

Mercury returns to your creative and romantic zone. You may feel playful and childlike; unfiltered communication can surface in a relationship. This energy will also be good for painting, poetry and music. Express yourself freely and you may find it balances and freshens your work and home duties.

Wednesday 12th

You could be moody today as things aren't going your way. It's possible that restless energy and the inability to use it makes you throw a tantrum or sulk. An evening alone may help you to withdraw from tension and realign with your true north. You may need to re-start a project.

Thursday 13th

The Moon in your sign makes you feel more like yourself and you get more inquisitive. Your mental activity is high and may be overflowing with creative ideas you would like to get off the ground soon. This could also be a good day for laughing until your belly hurts.

Friday 14th

A day of air energy can bring you more harmony, fun, love and compassion. Your heart may be wide open and willing to go the extra mile for someone special. Perhaps you can plan a trip together for some time in the future or research cultures that interest you.

Saturday 15th

You may be highly motivated and ready for a packed weekend. However, you may also choose to stay at home and enjoy your own environment. Hosting a party or event for friends might be a good idea if you can organise it with no hiccups or big egos clashing.

Sunday 16th

A need for security may conflict with your need to connect today. Your indecision may cause you to do nothing and drain your mental resources. Think about your daily routines, finances and private life. How much do you want to share? Perhaps you're being asked to open up a little.

Monday 17th

It's likely that you have scratched an old wound and you now have a sore spot. You may feel that you are doing more for others and not enough for yourself. If you think you are off track or being dragged from your comfort zone, re-assess where your time goes.

Tuesday 18th

You could be more outspoken today and can attempt to voice a few grievances. Look at what you might learn about yourself doing this. Friends and social groups may not be giving you the kick that you need right now, and you may feel you would be better valued elsewhere.

Wednesday 19th

A lover or creative project helps to balance some emotions that you aren't comfortable with. You could be extra assertive, which makes your self-expression shocking to some. If you wish to have your boundaries respected, then you must do the same for others. Don't dig bigger holes for yourself by speaking unkindly or without compassion.

Thursday 20th

Relationships may be tested now. You may not like someone probing too deeply but can communicate this positively and with strength. A partner may be more understanding than you think and would prefer to see you happy and balanced than stressed about where a relationship may be going.

Friday 21st

Use today to think about how much you are willing to share in a relationship. It may be that privacy is important as it keeps your heart guarded against disappointment. Try an unconditional approach to love and let your partner share a few things with you, too.

Saturday 22nd

More discussions may be needed in order to move on with a relationship. Family may offer well-meaning advice, but this could also conflict with your wish to be aligned with your truth. You may like to explain that if something doesn't feel right to you, there's no point spending energy on it.

Sunday 23rd

Saturn turns direct and can open up an area where you may have felt blocked. Travel opportunities may come up now. Settle something in your love life or accept things the way they are. The emphasis may now be on intense exchanges of serving each other's needs and may deepen your connection.

Monday 24th

A weight may be lifted from your mind as a decision is taken out of your hands. This could be the best resolution, as you're now happy to have emotional discussions and lay some ground rules for moving on. You can see the sense in this.

Tuesday 25th

A new moon and solar eclipse open a window of wildcard energy. This can be intensely loving, but also sexy and seductive. Stay open-minded and see where it leads over the next two weeks. Make sure that your schedule has time in it for intimacy and deep discussions.

Wednesday 26th

Thinking back to past times won't help and can re-open a wound you thought had healed. You may be feeling vulnerable now as you could be unused to this level of intensity in a relationship. Use your communication skills and get to the bottom of these feelings before they eat you up.

Thursday 27th

Emotions continue to flow, and you may be sharing your dreams and visions with a special someone. Discussions may motivate you to be your best self as this is your area of expertise. You may be dating this afternoon and step outside your comfort zone with a partner.

Friday 28th

Jupiter retrogrades into your career zone as if to tell you there is something you need to complete. This could come as an inconvenience but will ultimately bring you some bonuses. An open heart allows you to connect with groups who do great things for the wider world.

Saturday 29th

You may be tired today after the recent high levels of activity. However, you could also be rushing to make a deal or set something in stone with a partner. Slow down and know that there are many steps to take before signing a commitment. Time for deep introspection is coming.

Sunday 30th

Mars turns retrograde in your sign. This is a sign to take stock of what you have learned and make your pace easier for a few months. If you are highly motivated, you may find this time difficult or frustrating. Don't do anything impulsive simply for the sake of it.

Monday 31st

A measure of self-control might help you to deal with something that has been problematic in the workplace. You may have to be tough on someone or pull back on your many projects. Look at things from many different perspectives, use empathy and find a workable solution for all involved.

NOVEMBER
· · · · · · · · · · · · · · · · ·

Tuesday 1st

This is a challenging day and you may not get much done.
It may be an emotional rollercoaster where your busy mind
turns this way and that. Sharing, caring and privacy may be
the themes, as old wounds, maybe from being hurt in the past,
are re-opened.

Wednesday 2nd

You may experience a lack of energy and motivation today. Lines
of enquiry seem to lead nowhere. It may take some dedication
on your part to stick to one thing and follow it through. By
evening you may be much more flexible or wishing to spend
time alone on self-care and nostalgic thoughts.

Thursday 3rd

Another emotional but more productive day awaits. Using your
powers of investigation, you may discover avenues you would
like to explore more. These could be deep and mysterious
or psychological lessons, which could teach you more about
yourself and your reluctance to share your inner world with
someone special.

Friday 4th

Your inner compass directs you to dig up old behaviours and
get rid of them once and for all. This won't be a quick fix but
if you can dedicate yourself to some study or to accepting
spiritual guidance, you could embrace your psyche and pull
out the gold hidden within.

Saturday 5th

New groups may be a big help now. You may find collective
energy that suits where you are on your path. This may be a
karmic time, and you could have a visitor from the past. Be
warned, this could be an emotional trigger for you, but it has
come as a lesson.

Sunday 6th

The time has come to make plans to travel in a different way.
Listen to your inner voice and put your energy and motivation
into doing your personal inner work. Try not to be distracted
by voices of self-doubt. The deeper you go with this, the better.

Monday 7th

You might struggle today as you are keen to be left alone and
investigate your inner workings. Duties and obligations may
distract you. Maybe you can make a schedule to encompass all
you'd like to do and stick to it. Don't be seduced by projects
that are too big for you.

Tuesday 8th

A full moon and lunar eclipse light up parts of you that require
healing the most. Use your Gemini skills and research around
these issues before diving in headfirst. Take care that this
doesn't lead to stress or other health problems. Maybe you
need a trusted guide.

Wednesday 9th

Your inclination to speak without thinking may cause some
tension now. Somebody, maybe you, might speak out or expose
an old hurt that you thought you had dealt with. Take time to
process this before making any assumptions that may prevent
you from carrying on with your studies.

Thursday 10th

You could be pretty stubborn today and refuse to advance until others have acknowledged your current feelings. You may retract a favour or clash with authority. However, there is also the right kind of energy to realign with your true north and consider if you need to change your perspective.

Friday 11th

Blocks and restrictions may impede your progress today. The trick is not to take them personally. This may be a time to pause, reflect and review your progress so far. A rest stop on your journey may come to show you alternate routes or praise your efforts to date. Be gentle with yourself now.

Saturday 12th

If you are over-sensitive today, take a weekend off and spend time alone. This is a good time to snuggle down with a blanket and favourite movie or book. Escape into fantasy land for a while. The world will still be there waiting for you when you're ready to reconnect.

Sunday 13th

Stay in your safety zone and look around you. Do material things give you security? If you feel protected and nourished by your environment, don't change a thing. If items are taking up space that could be used for more quality, remove them. Make your space a home to be proud of.

Monday 14th

You may already be noticing the effect that your inner investigations are having. Getting to the bottom of your conditioned behaviours may help you to act differently when similar triggers come along. This afternoon you may be ready to put this to the test, but be mindful expressing yourself.

Tuesday 15th

Check in with your health and ensure that you haven't dismissed anything that needs exploring. This includes your mental health. Consider whether you're taking care of your own needs. Make time for a treat or a detox today.

Wednesday 16th

Venus enters your relationship zone, followed by your ruler Mercury. This heralds a time when you can express your desires and not feel ashamed. Ask for what you want, as you have more chance of getting it now. Think big and be bold enough to share with a partner.

Thursday 17th

If you are required to go through the details of a family event, you may find you feel resentful of this. You might be caught between partner time and family obligations. Do your duty and give everyone the benefit of your methodical and quick mind. Don't let others take advantage of your helpfulness.

Friday 18th

Tremors in your psyche may indicate that you are reacting to situations in your usual way. Remember that if you wish to heal and grow, this has to be changed. You may feel resentful about a person you perceive to be holding you back from your dreams or other activities. Take stock. Is that perception fair?

Saturday 19th

Today you may feel like throwing everything out and starting all over again. This isn't advised. See this as a test of patience. Talk to a partner or close friend and they may help you to find a reasonable workaround today. Be open-minded and ask for what you want. A good listener may be enough.

Sunday 20th

There is more air energy for you to access today. You may be more comfortable with this and can now get clarity and process things for yourself. There may have been insurmountable limits in your way, but you may now see why they were there. They may have prevented chaos.

Monday 21st

Apply more effort with your health today. An issue may have come to light recently and needs attention. You may begin to understand the deeper consequences this evening and give yourself a good talking to. A healthier diet or a better fitness regime may help you to stop bad habits.

Tuesday 22nd

The Sun moves into your partner zone now. Things could heat up, or you may have more of a yearning to get away and explore. You may now see how old habits and routines have let you down, or have accumulated so that they are now causing physical and emotional health issues.

Wednesday 23rd

You could be quite stubborn today and resist good advice. However, you may see sense and begin to put things in place for an easier transition. Emotions may be up and down as you navigate a new routine and try to see a different perspective.

Thursday 24th

Today comes with many blessings. Jupiter turns direct and eases the pressure at work and a new moon sets the standard for the next six months in your relationships. You may be experiencing more positive emotions and are able to discuss your needs with a partner. A corner has been turned.

Friday 25th

If you slip back to negative thinking, know that this is a quickly passing phase. Be willing to make a long-term plan for getting to know your body's needs. There's no rush to achieve anything right now, so take it slowly and get armed with all the information you need.

Saturday 26th

Stand as an observer to your own life and review what holds value for you. You may notice a shift in your thinking, and find that what was once important no longer is. Finances, joint investments and quality goods may be pushed aside in favour of deep investigation into what really makes you tick.

Sunday 27th

Your inner compass is asking if you are still aligned. Your true north may have moved slightly, but it is still there. An inner transformation may be taking place, whether you realise it or not. Spiritual movements may be attracting you and could give you some peace and fulfilment.

Monday 28th

If your mental energy seems lacking, try minimising your tasks and breaking them into bite-size pieces. You may be more outgoing today and willing to learn something new and unusual. However, you should do this gradually and avoid mental overload. This is a challenge for you as a Gemini.

Tuesday 29th

You may discover a person who can act as a guide or teacher on your path. You may now be ready to hear the answers to many of your questions. Try to be still and absorb what you are taught today. Process this before applying it to your life.

Wednesday 30th

A partner may be the one who shows up as your guiding light now. It's also likely that your shadow is making itself known and you are learning from your own deepest parts. What comes up now will be here to stay for the long-term and you must accommodate it.

DECEMBER
· · · · · · · · · · · · · · · · ·

Thursday 1st

This is a difficult day for reconciling masculine and feminine energies. You may be doing your best to bring together lovers or merging the lines of thinking and feeling. Hang on to your inner compass today and do what feels right to you. Honour your own values. Let everyone else see to their own business.

Friday 2nd

Don't talk yourself out of a good position now. You could be offered a great opportunity at work and you'd be foolish to turn it down. A partner is supportive and would like to see you expand and grow. Put something on paper and review what this could mean for you.

Saturday 3rd

Your social groups may be encouraging and there could be a lot of activity there today. They may look to you for leadership and you could find that they are strong allies when you have a personal decision to make. As a team, there are wheels to be put in motion now.

Sunday 4th

Neptune turns direct. If you were confused about your true north, you may have more clarity soon. Let the dust settle first. For now, look at your wants and needs and see if they have changed. Turn inwards and take time alone to find the clarity you seek.

Monday 5th

You may get a better sense of where your future lies ahead of you. A deep rumbling in your psyche may feel like a volcano waiting to explode, but think of it as furniture being rearranged. Some parts of you look better in the light, while others prefer to stay in the shade.

Tuesday 6th

A little voice of indecision whispers and you may falter today. Try to ignore your inner critic as you may be more inclined to self-doubt and low self-esteem. Look instead at the great work you've done this year and reward yourself. This evening a plan of action may be revealed.

Wednesday 7th

Your ruler, Mercury, has moved into your intimacy zone and is ready to look at how you share with others. You may find that you are more willing to commit to a joint venture now. This may keep your busy mind occupied and stimulated over the festive period.

Thursday 8th

Today there is a full moon in your sign. This is a time to look back at your achievements regarding how you present to the world. You may notice that you have no wish to rush around today and the outside world comes to you. This could be a moment of recognition.

Friday 9th

Challenges may feel like an attack of your values today and you may retreat to your safety zone. Your lover may ask more of you than you are willing to give. Likewise, work could be asking for finality. Don't get defensive, but ask for more time if you need it.

Saturday 10th

Strengthen yourself today by feeding your soul with things you love. A simple day at home surrounded by your treasures can help you to recharge and feel protected. Don't be tempted to follow an impulse to switch things up as you'll regret it later. Get ready to deepen a love interest.

Sunday 11th

Your heart may expand today as your inner compass points towards more joy and alignment at work. It may be that you have new duties that you are eager to get to grips with. Your safety zone may benefit from expanding your world view and accepting that you have much to learn.

Monday 12th

An outgoing mood may have you planning trips overseas or taking more of an interest in other cultures. Your partner may be keen to travel this journey with you. Try not to limit yourself and consider if you're the one restricting your own movements.

Tuesday 13th

When you have an idea in your head, you rush to make it real. Today you may be frustrated by the lack of momentum. Do what you do best and keep researching or gathering information in preparation. You may need to calm your impulses and let things play out in their own time.

Wednesday 14th

You may find it difficult to be your usual adaptable self today. There may be too many options to choose from or a lack of clarity that makes you stall. Check all the details and confer with family members who may be able to help you slow down.

Thursday 15th

Get grounded today and make your enquiries from a place of solid roots. You may have a lot of information to sort through, so a day of filing and organising may help to calm you. It will also be stimulating as you may find order in chaos. Throw away intangible ideas.

Friday 16th

It's possible that you feel overwhelmed today, so keep doing practical things. You may like to exercise or get out in nature as this could help. By evening you may have a better sense of balance, and find that thinking and feeling merge easily with creativity and romance.

Saturday 17th

Take a rest stop and allow yourself some quality time. A relationship may be a little suffocating, and you may need your own space today. You may be surprised by how a partner reacts to this, as they may need the same thing. Stay connected and honour each other's choices.

Sunday 18th

Your head and heart aren't in sync so you may escape to fantasy thinking or simply switch off and watch favourite movies. There may be something you would like to resolve but is out of your control right now. Leave it for another time when you may have more clarity.

Monday 19th

Deeply intense feelings may return you to a loved one now. This may be a past love or a current one with whom you wish to connect on another level. You may notice that old thought patterns are being replaced with new ones and positively changing the way you relate.

Tuesday 20th

A shift is happening within you and you may feel exposed or criticised. However, this is good for you and will help you incorporate new lessons you have learned this year. Your hopes and dreams may take a more meaningful turn and have more substance to them now.

Wednesday 21st

The winter solstice arrives, and you may feel like sharing it with someone special. Group celebrations may not be suitable as you may prefer to be quiet. This is a window of opportunity to set goals and intentions for the long winter nights ahead. Exploring the depths of your relationship may attract you.

Thursday 22nd

Let someone else lead you today. Take time to rest and pamper yourself before the festive activities take hold. A luxury or impulse buy just for you may satisfy a need. You can make time for others later, but today should be for you. Let yourself unwind and recharge.

Friday 23rd

Today's new moon is another chance to dedicate more effort into your intimate relationship. You may see a mountain ahead of you, but if you are determined not to rush, you may enjoy the journey and be at the summit gazing at the view with a very special person.

Saturday 24th

You could be on cloud nine today as a lover may have already swept you away and wooed you with words and gifts. Pleasant surprises await you and stir something deep inside. You may be in a particularly good place right now, so remember to give gratitude where it's due.

Sunday 25th

Your big heart may try to please everyone at once. There is a general feeling of goodwill on this festive day and for you, it stretches right from close friends to your bigger social groups. There is plenty of fun to be had today with your tribe.

Monday 26th

It's possible that you overdo the good things and don't feel like going anywhere today. This is fine and you mustn't feel guilty about it. You could feel irritable if asked to remember your duties and obligations, so do what you must and leave the rest for another time. Share the chores with others.

Tuesday 27th

You may have a lazy day and simply feel that switching off is in your best interests. Binge-watching festive movies or merging easily with loved ones will allow you to unwind but still be part of the team. Everyone can pull together if there's work to do.

Wednesday 28th

Special time with a lover may reveal what you both desire from the relationship. You may now have merged as a couple and share dreams and visions. This may make it easier for you to hold on to your inner compass, as you now have a mate to keep you steady.

Thursday 29th

Mercury turns retrograde today. This will let you review shared plans and finances, but remember to be clear in all your communications. There may be big plans within your social groups today and you want to be part of them. Get out and enjoy an event with your like-minded friends.

Friday 30th

Don't push against the collective today. You may have fleeting instances of energy, but overall, you may not have the strength to take on anything that requires assertiveness. Leave that for now and enjoy the slower pace of the day. Go along with the general flow of those around you.

Saturday 31st

If you don't want to join the party tonight, you don't have to.
The energy suggests that a quiet night at home with a lover,
close friend or by yourself could be the best way to end the
year. A celebration doesn't have to be big to be meaningful.
Have a wonderful close to 2022.

Gemini

....

PEOPLE WHO SHARE
YOUR SIGN

PEOPLE WHO
SHARE YOUR SIGN

The voices of Geminians are loud, clear and capable of moving mountains. Their influential and contagious words often have a global impact, whether it's a Tweet from former U.S. President Donald Trump or a song from Bob Dylan. Discover the Geminians who share your exact birthday and see if you can spot the similarities.

22nd May

Novak Djokovic (1987), Arturo Vidal (1987), Maggie Q (1979), Ginnifer Goodwin (1978), Naomi Campbell (1970), George Best (1946), Laurence Olivier (1907), Arthur Conan Doyle (1859)

23rd May

Ryan Coogler (1986), Richard Ayoade (1977), Manuela Schwesig (1974), George Osborne (1971), Melissa McBride (1965), Drew Carey (1958), Marvelous Marvin Hagler (1954), Joan Collins (1933), Rosemary Clooney (1928)

24th May

Joey Logano (1990), G-Eazy (1989), Dermot O'Leary (1973), Eric Cantona (1966), Rajdeep Sardesai (1965), Kristin Scott Thomas (1960), Priscilla Presley (1945), Patti LaBelle (1944), Bob Dylan (1941), Queen Victoria of the United Kingdom (1819)

25th May

Brec Bassinger (1999), Aly Raisman (1994), Roman Reigns (1985), Rasheeda (1982), Joe King (1980), Cillian Murphy (1976), Mike Myers (1963), Paul Weller (1958), Ian McKellen (1939)

26th May

Juan Cuadrado (1988), Scott Disick (1983), Lauryn Hill (1975), Helena Bonham Carter (1966), Lenny Kravitz (1964), Jeremy Corbyn (1949), Stevie Nicks (1948), John Wayne (1907)

27th May

Lily-Rose Depp (1999), André 3000 (1975), Jamie Oliver (1975), Paul Bettany (1971), Joseph Fiennes (1970), Paul Gascoigne (1967), Heston Blumenthal (1966), Henry Kissinger (1923), Christopher Lee (1922)

28th May

Cameron Boyce (1999), John Stones (1994), Carey Mulligan (1985), Jake Johnson (1978), Kylie Minogue (1968), John Fogerty (1945), Gladys Knight (1944)

29th May

Maika Monroe (1993), Riley Keough (1989), Melanie B (1975), Laverne Cox (1972), Noel Gallagher (1967), Carol Kirkwood (1962), La Toya Jackson (1956), Rebbie Jackson (1950), John F. Kennedy, U.S. President (1917)

30th May

Sean Giambrone (1999), Jake Short (1997), Jennifer Ellison (1983), Steven Gerrard (1980), Remy Ma (1980), Idina Menzel (1971), Mark Sheppard (1964)

31st May

Normani (1996), Azealia Banks (1991), Reggie Yates (1983), Colin Farrell (1976), Archie Panjabi (1972), Brooke Shields (1965), Lea Thompson (1961), Clint Eastwood (1930), Walt Whitman (1819)

1st June

Tom Holland (1996), Amy Schumer (1981), Alanis Morissette (1974), Heidi Klum (1973), Ronnie Wood (1947), Morgan Freeman (1937), Marilyn Monroe (1926)

2nd June

Sergio Agüero (1988), Morena Baccarin (1979), Dominic Cooper (1978), Justin Long (1978), Zachary Quinto (1977), A.J. Styles (1977), Wentworth Miller (1972), Andy Cohen (1968), Jeanine Pirro (1951), Charlie Watts (1941)

3rd June

Mario Götze (1992), Imogen Poots (1989), Michelle Keegan (1987), Rafael Nadal (1986), Anderson Cooper (1967), James Purefoy (1964), Susannah Constantine (1962), Allen Ginsberg (1926), Tony Curtis (1925), M. Karunanidhi (1924), King George V of the United Kingdom (1865)

4th June

Mackenzie Ziegler (2004), Lucky Blue Smith (1998), Brandon Jenner (1981), T.J. Miller (1981), Russell Brand (1975), Angelina Jolie (1975), Izabella Scorupco (1970)

5th June

Troye Sivan (1995), Amanda Crew (1986), Pete Wentz (1979), Nick Kroll (1978), Mark Wahlberg (1971), Ron Livingston (1967), Rick Riordan (1964), Kathleen Kennedy (1953), Ken Follett (1949)

6th June

Ryan Higa (1990), Natalie Morales-Rhodes (1972), Paul Giamatti (1967), Jason Isaacs (1963), Colin Quinn (1959), Björn Borg (1956), Sukarno, Indonesian President (1901), Thomas Mann (1875)

7th June

George Ezra (1993), Emily Ratajkowski (1991), Iggy Azalea (1990), Michael Cera (1988), Anna Kournikova (1981), Bill Hader (1978), Bear Grylls (1974), Prince (1958), Liam Neeson (1952), Tom Jones (1940)

8th June

Rosanna Pansino (1985), Javier Mascherano (1984), Kanye West (1977), Shilpa Shetty (1975), Julianna Margulies (1966), Tim Berners-Lee (1955), Bonnie Tyler (1951), Nancy Sinatra (1940), Joan Rivers (1933), Jerry Stiller (1927), Barbara Bush (1925)

9th June

Tanya Burr (1989), Mae Whitman (1988), Natalie Portman (1981), Matt Bellamy (1978), Miroslav Klose (1978), Johnny Depp (1963), Michael J. Fox (1961), Aaron Sorkin (1961)

10th June

Kate Upton (1992), Faith Evans (1973), Bill Burr (1968), Elizabeth Hurley (1965), Jeanne Tripplehorn (1963), Carlo Ancelotti (1959), Judy Garland (1922), Prince Philip, Duke of Edinburgh (1921)

11th June

Kodak Black (1997), Claire Holt (1988), Shia LaBeouf (1986), Joshua Jackson (1978), Peter Dinklage (1969), Hugh Laurie (1959), Gene Wilder (1933), Jacques Cousteau (1910)

12th June

Philippe Coutinho (1992), Dave Franco (1985), Kendra Wilkinson (1985), Adriana Lima (1981), Lil Duval (1977), Anne Frank (1929), George H. W. Bush, U.S. President (1924)

13th June

Aaron Taylor-Johnson (1990), Kat Dennings (1986), Mary-Kate and Ashley Olsen (1986), DJ Snake (1986), Chris Evans (1981), Steve-O (1974), Tim Allen (1953), Stellan Skarsgård (1951), W. B. Yeats (1865)

14th June

Jesy Nelson (1991), Lucy Hale (1989), Torrance Coombs (1983), Alan Carr (1976), Steffi Graf (1969), Boy George (1961), Donald Trump, U.S. President (1946), Che Guevara (1928)

15th June

Mohamed Salah (1992), Neil Patrick Harris (1973), Leah Remini (1970), Ice Cube (1969), Courteney Cox (1964), Helen Hunt (1963), Xi Jinping, General Secretary of the Communist Party of China (1953), Erik Erikson (1902)

16th June

John Newman (1990), Fernando Muslera (1986), Daniel Brühl (1978), Eddie Cibrian (1973), John Cho (1972), Tupac Shakur (1971), Jürgen Klopp (1967), Stan Laurel (1890), Geronimo (1829)

17th June

Kendrick Lamar (1987), Marie Avgeropoulos (1986), Venus Williams (1980), Sven Nys (1976), Tory Burch (1966), Greg Kinnear (1963), Barry Manilow (1943), M. C. Escher (1898), Igor Stravinsky (1882)

18th June

Willa Holland (1991), Pierre-Emerick Aubameyang (1989), Josh Dun (1988), Richard Madden (1986), Blake Shelton (1976), Isabella Rossellini (1952), Paul McCartney (1942), Delia Smith (1941), Barack Obama Sr. (1936)

19th June

KSI (1993), Macklemore (1983), Aidan Turner (1983), Zoe Saldana (1978), Laura Ingraham (1963), Paula Abdul (1962), Salman Rushdie (1947)

20th June

Christopher Mintz-Plasse (1989), Mike Birbiglia (1978),
Quinton Jackson (1978), Frank Lampard (1978), Roy Nelson
(1976), Mateusz Morawiecki, Polish Prime Minister (1968),
Nicole Kidman (1967), John Goodman (1952), Lionel Richie
(1949), Brian Wilson (1942)

21st June

Lana Del Rey (1985), Prince William, Duke of Cambridge
(1982), Brandon Flowers (1981), Chris Pratt (1979), Juliette
Lewis (1973), Joko Widodo, Indonesian President (1961),
Michel Platini (1955), Benazir Bhutto, Pakistani Prime
Minister (1953)